From the RUT to the LEDGE

The Story of One Family's Journey to Get Out of
Their Comfort Zone and Travel Around the World

SUZANNE RUTLEDGE

WESTBOW
P R E S S®
A DIVISION OF THOMAS NELSON
& ZONDERVAN

WestBow Press books may be ordered through booksellers or by contacting:

WestBow Press
A Division of Thomas Nelson & Zondervan
1663 Liberty Drive
Bloomington, IN 47403
www.westbowpress.com
1 (866) 928-1240

Cover design by Hannah Groseclose, cover image © Adobe Stock.

ISBN: 978-1-5127-9851-7 (sc)
ISBN: 978-1-5127-9853-1 (hc)
ISBN: 978-1-5127-9852-4 (e)

Library of Congress Control Number: 2017912481

Print information available on the last page.

WestBow Press rev. date: 09/07/2017

To my boys,
I'll adventure with you anywhere.

CONTENTS

PREFACE

Everyone loves a vacation, but not everyone loves travel. If you do love to travel—exploring and experiencing new and unfamiliar parts of the world—then it's usually part of the fabric of your being. It inspires and drives you, and you dream about the next trip before the current one is even complete. Instead of buying or receiving "things" at every holiday and special occasion, I prefer to collect experiences, and travel allows me to do exactly that.

The desire to explore new parts of the world is in my blood. It's who I am. And while some have no interest in traveling to far-flung and curious places, it gives me great pleasure and joy. And so it was, one might say, destiny that my husband Mitch, eight-year-old son Luke, and I would endeavor to travel all the way around the world.

Before the actual trip even begins, the planning and anticipation of a getaway gets my blood pumping. My curiosity is peaked when I plan to visit a new destination. I don't want the safety of the *known*, but rather the constant learning and newness of the *unknown*. How exhilarating it felt to plot multiple countries on our wall atlas and then take action!

This nine-month journey was truly a leap of faith and it proved to be the most meaningful and rich experience of our lives to date. I won't say it was a trip of a lifetime, because I know there will be another one. But, until then, I wanted to share our story and inspire *you* to take the leap, if your heart so desires. This is our story, but it includes many travel tips, discoveries, and details that can help make it your story, too. Our Reference and Recommendation Guide at the end of the book offers our favorite spots along the journey. We invite and encourage you to explore.

1

The Spark

Twenty years from now, you will be more disappointed by the things you didn't do than by the things you did do. So throw off the bowlines. Sail away from the safe harbor. Catch the trade winds in your sails. Explore. Dream. Discover.

—*Mark Twain*

The hazy sun had set as we bumped along in the darkness, the uneven roads making the rickety *tuk-tuk* feel like a homemade go-cart. Breathing in the sour exhaust, I thought to myself, *When am I going to put my foot down and stop appeasing Luke with these ridiculous tuk-tuk rides?*

The absence of delineated traffic lanes and lack of streetlights was only reinforced by the searing headlights of oncoming cars veering and honking their way through the crowded city of Delhi. We had landed in India just twenty-four hours before. My head ached from the stress and smog, and I willed us toward the hotel to a quiet retreat and soft bed.

I slid my arm around the shoulders of my eight year old. Our perspiring bodies were smashed together in the narrow, open backseat of the *tuk-tuk*, and he gleefully smiled at my husband and me before turning to stare out of the open cage. It filled my heart with joy to see such delight despite a long and trying day. No wonder I was a pushover.

As the driver slowed down to make the left-hand turn into the hotel's driveway, I saw a sedan careening toward us from the other direction, its lights blinding me. Why our inexperienced chauffeur thought he could make the turn in time, I'll never know, but as he pressed the gas and committed to the turn, I realized our small carriage was no match for this vehicle barreling toward us. The only thing between Luke's body and the rapidly approaching car was a flimsy bar of metal. We would surely be crushed.

I screamed and squeezed Luke into me as we narrowly missed being hit. As the *tuk-tuk* driver raced into the hotel's entrance and screeched to an unassuming halt, I wondered how many times we'd be saved from danger, or even death, on this journey around the world.

How do dreams become possibilities? What is the trigger that sets the unimaginable into reality? I have experienced pivotal moments in my life—moving away to college, marriage, and the birth of a child. But one warm November night, a significant moment changed the trajectory of my life and my family's lives. I didn't even realize it was a dream of mine until we spoke it into existence. It was the moment my husband and I looked at each other and said, "We can do that. Let's plan a trip around the world."

I've always had wanderlust and was fortunate to find that same quality in my husband, Mitch. While most young marrieds were honeymooning in Hawaii or the Caribbean, we set off for a road trip in Italy. It's not that we don't like the beach, but we found more excitement and adventure in exploring historical cities, eating, drinking, and learning more about each other's personalities by navigating foreign maps (before Google, how did we ever survive?). We spent ten days working our way from the Italian Riviera to Rome and loved every minute of it. While I had already tasted the sweet nectar of centuries-old Europe, this was Mitch's first trip. Looking back now, I'm so thankful he didn't run straight for the hills when I recall shouting Italian street names off an unwieldy paper map while he tried to return our rental car in central Rome. Our travel dreams could have been quashed in the first month of our marriage. But he's more tolerant than that, and the Italian honeymoon was what would become the first holiday of many spent abroad.

My best friend in high school, Kathrin, was half German. We met in German class, where she, of course, aced every test and carried me along in my ridiculous attempt at correct pronunciations. Her mother, from a small town in Southern Germany, was a tall and strikingly beautiful woman who spoke English with an exotic accent. Always dressed more stylishly than any of the other mothers, she made a statement with her dramatic scarves and classic, tailored trousers. Kathrin's mother met Kathrin's American father while he was serving in the military, and soon after they settled to raise their two children in the southern town of Marietta, Georgia. Each summer my girlfriend would take a trip to Deutschland to visit her mother's mother, Oma, and an extended family of aunts, uncles, and cousins. To my delight after our sophomore year, she invited me along to test out my mediocre German language skills and see the country shown in our textbooks in full Technicolor. I was thrilled!

My parents, both of whom had never been further than Mexico, were supportive as I applied for my first passport. My father had no interest in ever leaving the United States, although ironically his parents traveled to nearly every corner of the world on cruise ships well into their seventies. My mother never had much opportunity to leave America, but as it turned out, she had wanderlust too. In the years following my marriage, and faced with an empty nest, Mom began to go on church mission trips to numerous countries around the world.

In Germany, I had my first experience being outside the American bubble. Far away from my sheltered, middle-class family in the suburbs, I could spread my wings and kindle a lifelong love for exploration. I'll never forget the ease at which Kathrin and I moved through the beautiful cities of Heidelberg, Munich, and Würzburg that summer. Public buses and trains were not to be feared. The foreign language I learned actually meant something when I spoke it to people at restaurants and cafes. We were two young women enjoying the freedom and exploration of a different culture without a care in the world. We even hopped a twelve-hour bus to Paris for a few days! I'll never forget lying on top of the coverlet in our modest, un-air-conditioned budget hotel room, perspiring late into the night, but exhilarated to be seeing the world for the first time with the blinders fully off.

After my German excursion, due to my parents' disinterest in furthering my lust for all places outside America, I had to put my passion on hold until spring break of my senior year in college. This time I would spend a week in London. The trip reignited my obsession with Europe and uncovering the idiosyncrasies of a new culture. As I graduated from college, started my career, and began looking for someone to spend my life with, I knew a desire to travel had to be a common interest for us both. How wonderfully perfect that the man I fell in love with had never been outside of North America. But luckily, Mitch was willing and just as passionate about seeing the world.

After honeymooning in Italy, Mitch and I saved our pennies and vacation days so there could be more trips abroad. We were so enamored with Italy that we went again two years later, this time to Venice and south of Rome to the Amalfi Coast. As my German language skills had guided me through that country several years before, Mitch's many years of Latin helped us decipher Pompeii and Herculaneum. We found a common love of trying new foods (or being grossed out by them) and finding new wines and grapes we hadn't discovered in the Napa or Sonoma valleys of California. Mitch's parents had fostered in him an appreciation for art and museums, and we quickly sought out an audio guide wherever we went, making sure to synchronize our recordings so we could marvel and contemplate in unison. We were two nerdy lovebirds with headphones.

Desiring more than our limited annual vacations, we started to explore opportunities to actually work outside the United States. What better way to see the world than to live and work abroad full time?

I had begun my dream career in public relations a few years earlier at Coca-Cola Enterprises in Atlanta, while Mitch worked for a small software firm consulting with large retail companies. It was his company that offered us the opportunity to live overseas on the outskirts of London for two years.

Several expats who worked with Mitch recommended settling in Richmond, a small borough southwest of London. Still on the Tube line, Richmond offered easy access to one of Europe's grandest cities. Coca-Cola Enterprises also had an office just outside London, so I was fortunate to transfer within my department overseas. After selling our home and our cars and with only a few suitcases, we set off on the adventure that would spark a lifetime love of not just being tourists but explorers of the world.

While living in Europe, our entire view on life changed. We began to slowly peel away the American mantra of living for work and career and climbing the corporate ladder. We joyfully adopted the European lifestyle of working to live. What was once a complex puzzle of squeezing out vacations throughout the year with limited days became an accepted and encouraged five-week holiday! It was one of the greatest gifts we received when our zip code in Atlanta changed to a post code near London.

The more important and totally unexpected benefit of living, working, and exploring abroad was growing closer as a married couple. Without friends and family surrounding us, Mitch and I relied on each other more than ever to tackle the new culture, nuances to the language, and learning to drive on the opposite side of the road. We trained for a marathon together, planned weekend getaways, and learned what it was like to live and work in a foreign country. It was a blissful time as we enjoyed all that England and Western Europe had to offer. I found it hard to imagine returning home, so we contemplated extending our stay. But, ultimately we decided to return home to start a family. That was a dark time in my life, returning to the crush of American life, traffic, and commuting; and there was an endless social calendar of reuniting with friends and spending overdue quality time with family. I missed the freedom of living in a place where we knew few people and had no obligations except those we made for ourselves. It was a turning point when I realized I would rather live outside my home country than in it. The thrill of re-planting ourselves and discovering new experiences had become part of who I was, and I felt stifled in my homeland.

After our return to the States, we found it frustrating and ultimately impossible to pick up our old lives in Atlanta where we had left them, so we settled an hour away in the smaller university town of Athens, Georgia. We hadn't given up our dream of living abroad again, but we shifted our focus to starting a family and had a son the following year. Like a recurring dream, the travel bug never leaves you and within a year of Luke's birth we were off to South Africa. Sometimes new mothers receive a gift of jewelry from their husbands—I asked for two round trip tickets across the world.

We continued vacationing abroad as much as possible, but it's not as easy when you are leaving a toddler behind with his Nana. When Luke turned four, we decided to test the waters and take him along. We chose London since it was a direct flight from Atlanta, we were intimately familiar with the city, and would have low expectations of what we accomplished each day. Just walking the streets of my beloved former neighborhood and introducing it to my son would be a perfect vacation for me.

Traveling out of the country with children can make a parent fraught with concern; not just over logistics and jet lag, but also in wondering whether they'll enjoy and remember the international experience. I dreamt big with my expectations for our son. I wanted him to fall in love with the new culture, to embrace the food, activities, and people as I do.

After tedious research on how to have a successful overnight flight with a small child, we were thrilled to find that Luke embraced the transoceanic flight and adapted to the new culture with the same positive attitude that he has for most new things. After that successful first journey with child in tow, Mitch and I began dreaming of the next opportunity to live abroad and continue expanding our horizons and Luke's.

In November of 2014, Mitch and I were in Chile celebrating our fortieth birthdays (Luke was disappointed not to have been invited). We had survived the baby years and with our child happily enrolled in elementary school, it was time to celebrate us. We had settled into the comfortable routine of raising a family and we reveled in Luke's school performances, t-ball games, and swimming lessons. Parenting was more and more fun as the years progressed out of diapers and into the sweet spot of grade school. Life was very, very good, but the world outside our zip code was still calling us, beckoning another adventure beyond our comfort zone.

After a day of wine tasting in the Colchagua Valley of Central Chile, we met a young woman from Hong Kong who was staying at our small hotel. Over dinner, she shared that she was traveling around the world. Alone. For a year. I was so intrigued, I proceeded to pepper her with questions the rest of the evening. What had she learned? Was she ever scared? Had she packed too much? Had it been a positive experience? Resounding "yeses" and beautiful, colorful stories abounded. I was hooked and so was Mitch. It was like a switch had flipped on and I couldn't flip it back off. A revelation, actually. It was an idea that had never occurred to me—to travel for a period longer than a vacation, maybe even months at a time. Why had we never considered it?

It's worth mentioning that Mitch is the more logical, budget-minded leader of our home, and I keep us moving by planning vacations and dream experiences. He responsibly manages our finances, savings, and retirement accounts while I can barely balance a checkbook.

Mitch is also a huge advocate of setting goals for our marriage and our family and pushing us beyond our comforts and limits, even in the most everyday tasks. When we left our dinner with Selma that fateful night in Chile, we immediately started brainstorming ways that we, too, could travel around the world. So, the spark was ignited and the planning began.

2

What's Our Why?

When we were contemplating this trip, it was important for Mitch and me to determine why we were going to go, what our goals would be, and how long we would need to be away to reach them. I love learning about the world, its history, and its beauty. But instead of reading about it or watching it on film, it seems to stick with me and become part of my soul if I've witnessed it—touched, tasted, or smelled it. People fascinate me and visiting other cultures is a great way to understand the differences we all have, while appreciating the similarities that are innate in humankind. I wonder on a daily basis what is going on in the world outside of Athens. So, we travel to explore, live, and learn outside our comfort zone.

Turning forty years old also made me realize life is short. I want to live each day to the fullest and don't want to wait until "retirement," whatever that may look like, to travel extensively. I have watched several friends' parents work for decades, postponing their dreams and saving their money, only to see one of them succumb to cancer or some other debilitating ailment that prohibits travel. Suddenly, they live out their years with dreams unfulfilled. I didn't want to miss my chance to see the world.

But to travel aimlessly as tourists for months on end sounded exhausting and shallow. On a deeper level, our family loves to give back and serve others. We are involved in our community and church, feeding the homeless, and supporting college students through an outreach organization called Young Life. Although most of our travel had been for pleasure, I realized that as much as I love sightseeing, eating, and drinking my way through a new country, we can connect with people in a more meaningful way and build relationships if we volunteer where we visit. This isn't a new concept, just Google "voluntourism" and thousands of results pop up. But for us, it had to be a focal point of our around-the-world travel to make it worthwhile. We have been so blessed with everything in our lives and we have more than we need. Our hope was to serve others on this journey and make a small impact on those who are less fortunate. It would definitely stretch us, but that is what we intended to do.

For Mitch, our journey was also about creating lasting memories with our family. Some of his fondest memories of childhood started when he was about eight years old on road trips. Mitch's parents were diligent about taking his brother and him to interesting places. Trips to the Smithsonian museums in Washington, D.C.; Fredericksburg, Virginia; the California coast; the Spanish Galleon Museum in Key West, Florida; and the long car rides are a big part of his treasured childhood recollections. We were eager to make some of those memories as a family. Mitch and I believed Luke would remember this trip forever—not every detail necessarily—but the point was to have a family adventure.

Beyond adventure, Mitch hoped to give Luke a new perspective on the world. As parents, we want him to grow up with an open mind about people and places and encourage his curious spirit. We could all use a reset on our perspective of the world. So, we were excited to see what was happening not through the jaded, twenty-four-hour news channel lens, but to engage in real experiences with real people.

The title of this book alludes to another reason Mitch was inspired to take this journey. While being in a "rut" may be a bit harsh, "comfortable rut" is probably more accurate. We have a great life with wonderful people around us, stimulating jobs, and a vibrant community. Our routine is quite enjoyable, but Mitch believes in encouraging each other to try new things and keep our lives interesting. This trip was another great opportunity for us to get out of that comfort zone and challenge ourselves.

So, what does a trip like this look like? How do we invest enough in the places we visit, in the people, and the experiences to make it more like living and less like vacationing? We decided to travel slowly. If we had the luxury of weeks instead of days in one place at a time, we hoped it might allow us the opportunity to shop with the locals, understand a city beyond its tourist sites, and dig deeper into what makes each place unique. Pragmatically, we also knew that traveling slow would allow us the necessary time to homeschool Luke and set a pace of journeying that a seven year old could sustain.

"Separately, let's write down our wish list of destinations," Mitch suggested one evening. Our discussions after putting Luke to bed inevitably turned to our "RTW," round-the-world trip.

"If we each look at a map and write down everywhere we would go if we had nothing holding us back, then compare, we can see where there's overlap," Mitch continued. "That will give us a good starting point on how to build our itinerary." Always the methodical thinker.

So the next day after taking Luke to school, I scurried up to his bedroom where a world atlas hangs on the wall (yes . . . we *have* been influencing him since birth). With the world laid out before me, I started with New Zealand and worked my way westward, coming up with twenty-five stops. Wow. That could take awhile. How long are we going to be gone? Six months? Nine? A year? That would be tonight's discussion.

As it turned out, Mitch and I had lists that similarly overlapped. No surprise! We discussed narrowing the list to fifteen or twenty countries and traveling over a six-month period. There were many destinations on the list to which neither of us had traveled—Thailand, Vietnam, and Hong Kong to name a few. But we also included some of our favorites—Italy, France, and England. This would be an adventure of firsts but also a revisiting of the places where our wanderlust was born. We wanted to stretch ourselves outside of our travel comfort zone to experience completely new places but also integrate familiar territory to balance out the experience.

One of the first questions we considered after making our wish list was determining how to get there.

"I've been doing some research," Mitch confided one night, "and I think an around-the-world plane ticket won't give us the flexibility we want. You can only make a limited number of stops and they have to be in one direction—no backtracking."

He went on to explain, "I think the cost would be less and the choices greater if we flew with one-way tickets."

If Mitch knows anything, it's how to work the airlines. He has traveled weekly around the country on Delta Airlines since the start of his career and often reaches premium status as he racks up miles and then redeems them later for our vacation transportation. This, and the hotel status he earns, are the reasons I can happily say goodbye to him each week as he drives off to Hartsfield Jackson International Airport for his next business trip. I know with each mile that he travels, we are that much closer to free airline tickets or a hotel stay. We recommend investing in a credit card that brings you benefits. We love the Starwood American Express card for hotel point redemption and the Delta SkyMiles American Express card for airline travel rewards. Mitch also likes the Chase Sapphire Visa card, which converts dollars spent into redemption points of virtually any kind.

Not only does Mitch have a knack for squeezing the drops out of every earned mile and hotel stay, but he also has a knack for hacking. Travel hacking, that is. He follows several travel bloggers and websites and he has managed to digest and multiply their collective knowledge. Some of his favorites include Bootsnall.com,

Extra Pack of Peanuts podcast, and Nomadic Matt[1]. With their guidance and his crafty research, it is not unusual for him to supply me with a new credit card or two on a monthly basis. We go for the latest offerings of free miles for signing up and an additional 100,000 once you spend a certain amount. I file credit cards in my wallet like it's my job—and not a bad job either—spending money for double the pleasure!

We would end up purchasing our longest and most expensive tickets for the first leg of our journey to Auckland, New Zealand. Shockingly, all three cost less than $200 in total after earning the miles on United with their Visa credit card. Mitch continued hacking his way through our trip with multiple free flights and nearly thirty free nights in hotels with suite upgrades, free breakfast, and much more. He saw it as a hobby and challenge to work the system. I saw it as genius.

Now that we had an "open ticket" mentality and miles to cash in, we could build our itinerary. We jointly agreed that this was meant to be a warm weather journey. Why not avoid winter for a year if we could? This would mean we were traveling west, chasing summer. While we aren't beach bums, it certainly makes more sense when packing if you can avoid bulky sweaters and coats.

Our first stop would be the Southern Hemisphere, leaving behind the crisp and frosty Georgia mornings and traveling to New Zealand and Australia where spring would be in bloom. And our timing would work out well in helping us to avoid monsoon season in Southeast Asia. We would land there in the mild, but always sunny months of December and January.

To avoid crossing back into the Northern Hemisphere, we made the strategic decision not to include mainland China or Japan, where the bitter cold and rainy winter months would not jive with our flip-flops and t-shirts. In India, where summer temperatures can

---

[1] See Reference and Recommendation Guide for details on this and other favorites throughout the book!

reach 125 degrees Fahrenheit, the month of February hovers at a dry, dusty, and reasonable eighty-five. Heading south of the equator to Kenya in March would bring sunny skies and then we would continue around toward Europe for late spring and summer. It sounded like the perfect plan; a recipe for sunlight and blue skies. And we could pack layers and light jackets for the off chance we encountered cooler temperatures or light rain.

Of course, this was just the outline. Planned, structured, and Type-A to the core, even I appreciated the importance of some flexibility in the plan. We weren't ready to commit to certain countries until closer to the time we would arrive. Egypt, Turkey, and Israel are places we had always wanted to go, but we were not willing to take a child into a war zone or politically hostile area. The one-way tickets again turned out to be the right choice for us so that we could monitor current events and make a real-time decision as to our next destination. But for my sanity, we decided to make reservations for the first two months. This allowed us to enjoy our travels before having to hunker down and plan the next leg.

Of course, a critical piece of this journey, or any trip for that matter, is the budget. How much were we willing to spend on this experience? And how would we pay for it? Mitch and I had started a travel fund early in our marriage—a separate bank account where we squirreled away a monthly amount for vacations and travel. We also made a deliberate choice to dip into our life savings for this monumental experience.

While some people spend extra income on a boat, a fancy car, or a vacation home, we had chosen to spend it traveling the world. It was an important investment to us and we trusted that the return would be an enrichment of our lives.

Mitch and I determined a reasonable monthly cost of living and agreed to stay in mid-range priced accommodations. We knew some countries, like Australia and New Zealand, would be more expensive than Southeast Asia, so we expected the budget to ebb and flow, but it would hopefully average out to our planned $5,000 per month.

With our budget set and our vision defined, we began putting the plans into motion. Our budget allowed for a nine-month journey, but we would have to find someone to rent our home in Athens. Paying a mortgage and traveling without our income was not sustainable. Finding a renter could be tricky, considering we weren't yet ready to share publicly that we were considering this journey. It had to be done quietly, but how?

One morning at church, I passed a dear friend in the stairwell. She and her husband were our first friends in Athens and I had known them since college. They made the leap from Atlanta to Athens several years before us and helped pave our way by introducing us to friends, our church, and our neighborhood.

"Suzanne, I need you to keep your ears open for me," Rebecca requested as we passed, each with children pulling our arms in the opposite direction. "Kevin and I are finally ready to renovate our house and we need a place to live, but I can't find anything that's not student housing or in the next county. Let me know if you hear of anyone with a good rental for us in the area."

Did I just hear her correctly? Could it really be this easy? I rushed home and recounted the conversation to Mitch, who had just returned home from a weekend with friends in Atlanta.

"You will never guess what Rebecca said to me today at church." I repeated the conversation. "Do you think *they* could be our renters? Should we offer our house to them?" My wheels were already turning and I was mentally packing my bags.

"Suzanne, wait a minute," my other half and voice of reason responded. "We have no idea how many months they will need a house or when they want to start construction. Let's slow down a bit."

"That's fair," I countered. "Let's pray about it for two weeks and see where we land." This is my tried-and-true response to anything Mitch says that I don't immediately agree with. In all fairness, I'm not trying to pull a fast one. I genuinely believe that doors open and close because God has a plan for your life. I was willing to give Him time to crack it open a bit more or slam it in our faces. To my delight, the sunlight poured through the opening and two weeks later, Mitch was having lunch with Kevin and offering our home.

With friends willing to rent our house for nine months while we were away, our plans gained momentum. We now considered our jobs and decided requesting a leave of absence was appropriate. Mitch's company is consistently ranked as one of the best companies to work for in the country because of their employee-friendly policies and programs. While a nine-month sabbatical wasn't one of them, Mitch reasoned they would be open-minded. And they were. Because I worked part-time as a contractor for a public relations and marketing agency, I had to resign. However, I did so with a pleasant and truthful discussion in the hopes that I could return if there was still work for me after our trip.

"Are you awake?" I asked Mitch quietly as he lay beside me one night.

"Yes," he answered in a hushed tone that intimated he was not ready for a long conversation.

"Are we doing the right thing?" I wondered aloud. "I have an anxious stomach whenever I stop and consider what we are doing—quitting our jobs, leaving our home, keeping Luke safe while we travel. What if he doesn't want to go?"

We hadn't really considered whether Luke would or would not want to take this trip. As an only child, he has always considered himself part of a team of three rather than the subordinate, which requires constant reminders and discipline—we are not a democracy.

Luke met the news of our trip around the world with excitement, enthusiasm, and not a bit of trepidation. Definitely my genes! He is enrolled at a local private school and we weren't sure what the administration's position would be on extracting him from second grade. I am not an educator by trade. (God bless teachers. I don't know how they do it.) But with the resources online, I believed I could homeschool Luke during our travels without causing any permanent damage. Luckily we weren't talking physics or advanced calculus.

We scheduled a meeting with the headmaster and Luke's teacher to obtain their approval; however, since the wheels were already in motion for this trip there was no turning back regardless of their reaction. Still, a part of me thought without the blessing of his school, we might be deemed irresponsible parents if we skipped the country with a seven year old.

"You probably don't know this about me," remarked Headmaster Thorsen after we stated our case, "but I have spent my life traveling around the world. I think I've been to more than forty countries so far. I can think of nothing better than exposing Luke to different cultures and countries. You can absolutely go with our blessing."

Seriously? Another threshold so easily crossed? The door was swinging wide open and we were running through it. The pieces of this puzzle were coming together. Telling some members of our family, however, was met with significantly less enthusiasm.

"I'd rather be drowned in a bathtub than travel around the world for nine months."

My sister never minces words. As a mother of four girls, she is always ripe with a hint of sarcasm and drama. She breaks out in hives at the thought of getting on an airplane, so it was no surprise that she couldn't fathom our plans.

"I mean," she said backpedalling, "that's great for you. I'm sure you will have an incredible time. I just can't imagine doing something like that myself."

Fair enough. Traveling, much less long-term traveling, isn't for everyone. I get it. As we began to tell our family and friends, there were some who were thrilled for us, some intrigued, and some downright perplexed. My mom was ready to climb into my suitcase and that sentiment was heart-warming. But I also understood those who wished us well and scratched their heads. As the days drew nearer for us to depart, we were overwhelmed with kindness and well wishes from everyone regardless of their initial reaction. So much so that it made it hard to leave our beloved Athens. But we did.

TRIP TIP: Download the Skyscanner app for the easiest platform to search all airlines around the world at once for the best prices and availability.

3

Packing One Bag . . .
for Nine Months

Before we could lift off on that first flight from the United States, we had some packing to do. Besides clearing out our personal belongings in our home to make room for the renters, we were feverishly researching and buying all the necessary items for our bags, including the suitcases themselves.

With our relatively weak lower backs and general distaste for being labeled "middle-aged backpackers," Mitch and I tried out multiple small, soft-sided rolling bags. Our hope was to purchase a bag small enough to carry onto most flights, barring those budget airlines in Europe and Asia where that's next to impossible. In the end, we realized that with the necessary liquids needed for a family over a period of months (versus a typical one-week vacation), checking bags would be required more often than we had originally hoped. But at least our suitcases didn't lend themselves to over-packing and thus we were able to avoid bag fees. After many test packs and rolls around our house, we decided on the PacSafe twenty-two-inch rollers and they were fantastic.

Upon learning about our trip, many girlfriends immediately asked, "How in the world do you pack for nine months?"

The answer is simple; you pack for one week. With the help of my favorite packing accessories, Bago travel cubes, we rolled our warm weather attire into brightly-colored "sausages." My scarf would pull double-duty as a bathing suit cover-up, my flip-flops universally working as beach shoes or shower thongs. Mitch invested in thin, but expensive, merino wool shirts and socks, having found this recommendation during his travel blog research. Merino takes wear and tear much better than cotton t-shirts and typical workout socks—who knew? Luke reveled in the idea of trading in his school uniform for quick-dry athletic shorts and shirts and what kid wouldn't love wearing the same clothes repeatedly day in and out until we found a washing machine?

Despite our best efforts, we packed too much. I insisted on including a dressy top for those few and far between nights out on the town. And how could I leave behind my favorite pair of jeans even if they were the bulkiest item in the bag? In the end, we would have to purge a few unnecessary items, so our general rule of thumb became simplicity and re-wear. I now abide by the 5-4-3-2-1 rule, no matter the length of my trip:

5: Five tops (t-shirts, long-sleeved shirt, and a thin, pullover fleece)
4: Four bottoms (skort, maxi skirt, trousers, and jeans)
3: Three shoes (comfortable walking sneakers, flip-flops, and flats)
2: Two swimsuits
1: One lightweight rain jacket and one dress

It turned out the jeans were a great choice and I wore them often. The dressy top, not so much. I quickly determined which shirts were my favorites and once they were worn out, I bought new ones in street markets or European stores several months later. Only one top made it all the way around the world with me, and I still have that gray t-shirt hanging in my closet. I may never throw it away!

As a homeowner, there seem to be a million details that must be tied up neatly before you leave the country for almost a year. Mitch has always managed our banking and utilities online, so I minimized our snail mail to virtually nothing by cancelling every catalog and putting all of our magazine subscriptions on hold. Mitch researched our mobile phone options, and we determined that a global package with T-Mobile was the best option for him. I no longer had a plan with my carrier, instead relying on Wi-Fi connections and utilizing FaceTime and text to connect with family.

As our departure date grew closer, our packing and planning grew to a feverish pace. The house became more disheveled as we attempted to tidy and pack away our belongings. Because we were renting to friends, it made the job a lot easier. All of our furniture remained in its place, as well as the majority of the kitchen and its contents. We packed up our clothes, linens, and personal items and stored them in our unfinished basement.

The more we tried to minimize our baggage while packing, the more we thought of things we needed or thought we might need during the long journey. What was surely needed were thoughtfully-crafted goals for our trip. After some reflection and conversations with friends, I came up with three, beyond staying healthy, safe, and sane.

I am in the business of public relations, telling the positive and compelling stories of other companies and brands. Rather than long-form writing, I am often pitching story *ideas* to journalists and editors. It's a finely-tuned skill and a fun challenge. I get a true rush from drafting that perfectly-worded email hook that garners the attention of a reporter who receives thousands of inquiries, story pitches, and newsletters a day.

On our journey, I wanted to do both—craft an interesting and well-written article and then pitch it to a travel or parenting publication. My goals were not huge, just one story in print about our adventure. And I knew that I would find inspiration and story ideas along the way. So that was Goal #1.

Secondly, on the advice of a friend, I decided to read a book set in each country we were visiting. As an avid reader without a lot of time to cozy up with a good book, I thought these nine months would be filled with opportunities on planes, trains, and beaches to plow through several novels. Without my monthly book club gatherings with friends, this goal would drive me to keep reading while finding relevant stories within our travel destinations. Rather than weigh down my bag with paperbacks, the Kindle my parents gave me as an early birthday gift held hundreds of books in one slim, easy traveling device.

My final goal was to visit all seven continents—a goal that came about early in the planning process to fulfill a dream of mine. I had been to six continents during previous trips, but had yet to add Australia to the list.

Beyond our goals, we had a few priorities that were required during the trip. Most importantly was progressing our child through second grade. With the school's blessing, we packed up Luke's math and handwriting books, and I downloaded spelling lists for the remainder of the year. On Luke's Kindle, Mitch downloaded the entire series of 190 Hardy Boys mystery books and we promised Luke's teachers he would learn multiplication and cursive handwriting. Focusing on reading, writing, and arithmetic was all they asked since they knew he would have the world as his classroom.

As our departure date quickly approached, a constant nervous stomach and anxiety set in. I was now regularly (and silently) questioning whether our decision to leave was the right one, all the while knowing that we had thoughtfully and carefully planned this journey. Mitch and I didn't discuss it, but I wondered if he felt nervous, too. I tried to reassure myself that we were not plowing headstrong into an uncertain future. We were being led through open doors that were answered prayers.

Ten years before, when I fretted about moving abroad to London, I lived and breathed a Bible verse that, to this day, is my mantra, "*Do not be anxious about anything, but in everything, by prayer and petition with thanksgiving, present your requests to God. And the peace of God that transcends all understanding will guard your hearts and minds in Christ Jesus."* (Amplified Bible, Phil. 4:6-7)

I knew in my heart of hearts that if God was for this journey and I trusted that He had blessed this request of ours, that I should thank Him and trust that He had it under control. It was a gift from Him that I shouldn't belittle with worrying. To make the most of it, I needed to have faith that we were doing the right thing because He was making it possible. I relied on that faith throughout the trip whenever I was confronted with a situation or event that might normally cause fear and angst.

A funny thing happens when you move away or exit your "home life" for an extended amount of time. Everyone you know wants to see you and say goodbye. In our busy lives of careers, raising kids, and the myriad of activities our families undertake each week, there's little room left for socializing. Sure, we see friends in the carpool line and in the baseball field parking lots, but quality time for adult friends becomes a lower priority. Until you are leaving. The urgency is suddenly there, and it's a mad dash to find a date on the calendar to spend time with every friend group you have. So, we spent our final weekends seeing college friends, family, extended family, church friends, and even managed to squeeze in an early eighth birthday party for Luke. It was madness, but it was also such a sweet and memorable time with people we love and who were supporting us.

TRIP TIP: Join the community of around-the-world travelers online. There are travel blogs (like ours!), podcasts, and websites that provide excellent, concrete details and advice from individuals and families who have already journeyed around the world.

4

New Zealand: Off We Go!

My mother dropped us off at Hartsfield Jackson International Airport and we found ourselves amongst thousands of other busy travelers. I have always loved airports and the anticipation they bring of new adventures. I enjoy walking down the long concourses and reading the destination signs on each airline's departure board. Familiar cities or faraway lands in every corner of the globe beckon me to visit again or discover them anew. I love to make mental wish lists for future journeys as I pull my carry-on down the freshly-waxed walkway. When I encounter destinations I never knew existed (Baotou, Bengaluru, and Busan!), I am once again reminded just how many places there are in the world to explore. Nine months would have to be the beginning of a never-ending lifelong expedition of the globe. This was not what some called, "the trip of a lifetime," but rather, "one chapter in a lifetime of exploration."

Stepping onto the airplane was a conscious moment of deliberate remembrance. We had come so far, dreaming and planning, and now it was officially reality. There was excitement, anxiety, fear, and euphoria all mixed into one large pre-flight cocktail. Mitch was slightly somber and stressed out anticipating twenty-two hours of being cramped into a coach class coffin-like seat. You can only mentally prepare so much for folding your six-foot-six lanky body into a space more appropriately built for a child.

Enthusiastically, Luke bounded into his seat (just as he would on every leg of our journey) and excitedly pressed his face to the window. I found myself in the middle. Literally. Stuck between my boys who would fitfully cheer and complain as we initially completed crossing our continent and then the vast Pacific. I reminded them both, and myself, that we could survive this passage.

I reconsidered my confidence fifteen hours into our journey. Somewhere over the Pacific, our airplane started to bounce. And by bounce, I mean flutter violently up and down, side to side with such extreme wildness that I felt sure our journey was over before it had even begun. I jolted awake from my half-slumber and grabbed Mitch's hand. Luke was snuggled up in his cotton sleep sack at our feet, finding that the floor space of three seats across was the perfect length for him to stretch out and sleep. He was oblivious to our seemingly near-death experience.

As I clutched Mitch's fingers with wide-eyed terror, I remembered a friend telling me of her journey with two small children to New Zealand and how, "after the treacherous flight, I swore I would never go back." Could this be normal? Maybe it was just an orientation to the South Pacific, our first test of guts and strength. If so, I felt truly sorry for the flight crew who endured it on a weekly basis. This was horrible.

After what seemed like an hour, the wind gods stopped toying with our 747, and we settled into the final hours of our flight. But it wasn't our last leg. We landed in Sydney for a twelve-hour layover, then finally boarded our connecting flight to Auckland, New Zealand—the actual first stop on our multi-country tour. What we knew would be a painfully long, multi-leg crossing of the globe was bearable because it was mixed with excitement and anticipation. And it was only one way! Luckily, we would not journey this path again. From this day forward, we would (mostly) head west, and our flights would become significantly shorter as we went.

And, there was much to celebrate. When we landed in Sydney we slid into the American Express lounge, thanks to Mitch, our travel hacker, and poured two glasses of champagne. Jetlag could not slow down our penchant to toast the beginning of what was to come. And I had achieved a little milestone of my own, reaching my personal Goal #3. In touching down in Australia I visited my seventh (and final) continent.

When you are offered the opportunity to go to Antarctica, it could be your chance to see all seven continents. At least that's what I thought when I was asked to go with Coca-Cola in 2003. I was working at the time for Coca-Cola Enterprises—the job that established my career and taught me the fundamentals of writing, media relations, and most importantly . . . how to follow my dreams. It was in this role that I was offered a leadership opportunity to join forty-nine other Coca-Cola employees from around the world on a three-week expedition to the Antarctic. Led by renowned explorer Robert Swan, it was one of the company's first public forays into environmental leadership and sustainability. What had always been a local effort to better recycling, water conservation, and lower energy consumption was morphing into what would become a global initiative for The Coca-Cola Company and its bottlers, and I was privileged to join the first leadership team.

The exhilaration I felt upon learning I was part of that expedition was akin to what I felt when we landed in Australia and New Zealand. Far away from home in an unknown environment, I was giddy with anticipation about what our family would experience and learn from this new and exotic destination.

Sometimes the most mundane activities feel special and different when done in a new place. Walking down unfamiliar streets, navigating a foreign grocery store; these are things that challenge you when living somewhere new. Our apartment in the Northcote Point neighborhood of Auckland was probably very standard, possibly even dull, from a New Zealand resident's point of view. We found it to be magical. Set on the harbor, our street was warmed by the spring Southern Hemisphere sun and cooled by the breezes blown in from the Pacific Ocean. To overcome our jetlag, we prepared no agenda and spent our first days simply walking the neighborhood streets.

I strive to be content with how much or how little God provides for us, trusting that He will always take care of us. As we walked under the piercing blue sky past gardens popping with pink rhododendrons waking to spring, I was overwhelmed as I recognized this journey as an abundant gift from Him. He'd given us so much already and we had nine more months of adventure in front of us. At the same time, we had physically removed a lot out of our lives. With only a few clothes and necessary personal items, we had let go of so much that was part of our daily, comfortable routine. We challenged ourselves to clear out the clutter and make more space for experiences and encounters. We were doing this tangibly by paring down all that we owned to just one carry-on and one small backpack each, but also by releasing the busyness of our lives and opening ourselves up to a slower pace. Getting rid of our "stuff" forced us to look up and around at what God had created.

It's funny how the first place you visit on a multi-stop trip seems to immediately be your favorite, since there is nothing yet to which you can compare. We embraced Auckland and found it to be charming and beautiful, if not a bit quiet. The entire North Island has only 3.5 million residents and Auckland a mere 1.4 million, so the downtown streets felt strangely sparse to be the most populated city in the country. We sometimes felt like we had missed "the big event" and everyone was gathered elsewhere. We took to the ferryboats and traveled around the islands, exploring the vast green hillsides and quaint harbor towns that make up the region.

One of my favorite excursions was the day we chose to visit Waiheke Island. We were reminded of the adventure that life has in store when you take advantage of "unique" forms of public transportation. We hopped the ferry under a brilliant blue sky to the island known for its wine, gleefully anticipating a day in the sun and tasting the local varietals. Mitch and I found early on in our relationship that we have a mutual love for exploring wine regions, not just for tasting, but learning about the history and viticulture of the area. We make it a point to seek out a winery and learn about the local grapes, and that became a fun, adult part of our family trip that we could share together. Mitch made sure that each winery was a science or math lesson for Luke, and he sat patiently while we tasted.

After disembarking the ferry, we hopped the local bus and it carried us up into the hills to our first winery, Cable Bay Vineyard. Only the local bus never seems to drop you right where you need to be. We walked a few *miles* before reaching the tasting room, but that made the first sip all that much better.

From there, we walked to another nearby and well-reputed winery, Mudbrick. Along the road, spring was in full bloom and we smelled the sweet essence of honeysuckle. I stopped to pull off a flower and after gently pinching the end, pulled a small drop of nectar to my lips.

"Wow!" Luke exclaimed. "Is that honey?"

Had I never taught my child about honeysuckles? These vines drape themselves throughout our forested backyard at home. My mother and grandmother taught me about the sweet snack in the woods when I was Luke's age. How had I never taken the time to introduce him to this lovely plant?

"Yes, the best kind," I responded. We plucked a few together and I taught him how to extract the juice. He smiled and continued pulling them from the roadside vines throughout the afternoon. It was the first of many precious moments I would fondly remember from the trip. Apparently at home I was too busy or unwilling to stop and eat honeysuckles. Well, that was all about to change.

There were a lot of firsts during our two-week stay in New Zealand, which made sense considering it was our testing ground for the months to come. In Auckland, we discovered MOTAT, one of many transportation museums, which delighted Luke for hours. I had no idea this vast world held so many science and transportation museums. The things you learn when you are a boy's mother!

We also began to learn how far our dollars would stretch. New

Zealand is not cheap, so we spent most nights cooking in our rented apartment and eating homemade sandwiches as picnics for lunch. I quickly grew aware of how much I overeat at home simply because it's available to me. With a limited budget and no access to a full pantry, I found my stomach shrinking and a humbling realization of my former gluttony.

Perhaps my favorite lesson learned in New Zealand was our most uncomfortable. We drove down to Napier, a small beach town known for its 1920's art deco architecture and beautiful seaside promenades. We rented bicycles and explored more wineries along the coast. It was difficult to find any accommodation within our budget, so we decided to try our luck at a hostel. Mitch and I had never backpacked before, both having missed out on post-college, low-budget travel through Europe and finding ourselves too old and unwilling to stay in hostels when we lived abroad. But now seemed like the right time to try it out. After reading positive and inspiring reviews online, we booked three nights at the YHA in Napier.

It was there that we were stretched out of our comfort zone for the first time on the trip. It wasn't the twenty-two-hour flight and life-threatening turbulence or driving on the opposite side of the road through winding mountain highways (as the shotgun passenger I was still trying to recover from the anxiety of having no control over the vehicle while sitting in what my brain told me was the driver's seat). It was the three nights in the hostel that reminded me what a pampered, middle-class, middle-age softie I am. Mitch and me both. Of course, Luke never batted an eye. He loved sleeping on the top bunk bed and paid no mind to the prison cell-sized room or the constant smell of burning food coming from the kitchen just below us. We suffered through and accepted our fate as budget travelers with limits. If there was ever any doubt, it was official— we are not communal bathroom-types. But, we were light hearted enough to laugh it off and mention it fondly throughout our trip as "the worst place we ever laid our heads."

As we walked along the promenade one evening watching

the intense waves crashing along the shoreline, I began picking up stones along the beach. Rather than fine sand, this and many other beaches across the world have smooth oval-shaped stones in shades of black and gray. As I rolled one over in my palm, I knew this was a reminder that we, too, were being worn down, smoothed to something more beautiful. The waves may continue to crash— surprising and sometimes frightening us—but the result would be something more refined and resplendent after months and months of experiences.

Before we knew it two weeks had passed and we were off again. This time we boarded a shorter flight to see familiar faces in Melbourne, Australia.

TRIP TIP: Our families at home had more peace of mind knowing we were registered in the STEP program with the U.S. State Department. Their Smart Traveler app allows you to easily document details of when and where you will be in case of an emergency in that country.

5

Australia: G'Day Mates!

Melbourne, Australia, is consistently voted the "Most Livable City in the World" and our dear friends who are American and South African expats whole-heartedly agree. They welcomed us into their homes and community and from the start I felt as if we were on a recruitment visit. I could relate to the pride and constant praise of Melbourne because I cheer just as loudly about our hometown of Athens. I appreciate the positive excitement that residents exude when they love where they live; so it was fun diving into their everyday lives and experiencing the culture and laid-back lifestyle they had come to enjoy "down under."

We intentionally planned our itinerary to include a stop with friends in the first month of our tour. The similarities between Australia and the United States are numerous, and we enjoyed easing into our foreign surroundings without being completely jolted by vastly different cultures and practices. We were also excited for Luke to have friends his own age to play with and our friends were eager to include him in their kids' lives and activities right away. Just two days into our visit Luke celebrated his eighth birthday, and they graciously threw a party for him at their favorite indoor, wall-climbing attraction. Continuing our theme of wine discovery, one weekend we all day-tripped out to the Yarra Valley for various tastings, lunch, and a stop at the most decadent and whimsical chocolate shop I had ever seen. Despite already missing our friends and relatives back home, we enjoyed this as the first of several visits with friends around the world.

Since we were homeschooling Luke, Mitch had the clever idea to immerse him into other classrooms around the world. We hoped it would be an opportunity for him to see what second graders learned in other countries, and it might also open his eyes to the various ways of teaching and learning. Melbourne was the perfect test case for our extra-curricular classroom concept because our friends' children attended a lovely neighborhood school within walking distance of their home. Having pre-arranged our visit with the headmaster, Luke borrowed a school uniform shirt and eagerly joined the girls for a day at primary school. I wondered if he would feel uncomfortable or stick it out the entire day, but with Chloe by his side he happily integrated into Miss Cotter's classroom and found that most things were similar to his school at home. Recess was still his favorite part of the day!

A stop in Melbourne is just not complete without a few days on the Great Ocean Road. In my ignorance, I had never known about this natural wonder, but our friends educated us quickly. They promised that it would be one of the highlights of our visit and it was. The Great Ocean Road is a three-hour drive heading southwest from the city, so our kind and brave friend allowed us to borrow his SUV for the two-day excursion. As the city and population melted away, the drive became curvy. As we reached the coast, the stunning ocean-side cliffs came into view. The captivating scenery was a hybrid of the Northern California coast, the Cliffs of Moher in Ireland, and Italy's Amalfi Coast.

We stopped in several small towns to watch surfers brave the crystal blue waters and to glimpse koalas, tropical birds, and waterfalls in the forested mountains along the shore. Rounding one corner along the windy road we happened upon a beach inlet covered in smooth stones. Amazingly, this spot was being transformed into a stacked stone sanctuary with tall piles of large rocks reaching toward the sky like a miniature cityscape. Mitch and Luke created a pillar alongside other visitors and we lingered for a long time, sensing the remarkable, almost spiritual, peace that the shoreline provided against the backdrop of the endless blue sea beyond.

Our final destination before turning back toward Melbourne was the Twelve Apostles. The stormy Southern Ocean and blasting winds had gradually eaten away at the softer limestone, forming caves in the cliffs. The caves eventually formed arches and when they collapsed, twelve rugged rock stacks, more than 100 feet high, were left isolated from the shore. Just eight structures remain because of continued erosion and the majestic rock formations jutting out from the ocean's surface were magical to behold. As the road meandered back toward civilization, we were all silent as we soaked in the views and the realization that we had just seen the first of many breathtaking wonders in Australia that only God in nature could create.

Upon our return home people asked us hundreds of times, "What was your favorite place you visited?" The Great Barrier Reef in Australia was nearly always our response. Granted, that is a tricky question considering all we saw and did, but there is something about the extraordinary beauty under the sea that found us completely awestruck.

Since the reef stretches more than 1,400 miles along the northeastern coast of Australia, there are many jumping off points if you want to explore underwater. We flew into Cairns and boarded a two-day, one-night budget excursion for snorkeling and scuba diving. In the early morning hours, we walked along the pier to find our boat among many headed out with tourists; every passenger ready to tackle a bucket-list dream. A smaller boat carried us out of the bay and after an hour we met up with a larger, live-aboard cruiser that would be our home for the night floating over Norman Reef.

Luke was immediately smitten with the staff who were young, funny, and eager to teach him the basics of breathing with a mask and snorkel and finding flippers to fit his little feet. Since only Mitch was scuba certified and Luke was still too young to learn, he and I became snorkeling partners and Mitch joined us when he took breaks from diving.

The sun shone brightly as we shimmied out to the back platform of the boat and slid into the warm, turquoise water. Mouths tightly wound around our snorkels, Luke and I held hands as he steadied his heartbeat. Breathing deeply, we both tilted our heads downward into the sea. This was a test for Luke, his first attempt at snorkeling. But it was also the first of what would be many adventurous excursions on our trip. We knew our child might need some encouragement, but he was usually willing to take risks. I held my breath and waited to see if he, too, had the desire and will to go out on the ledge.

A whole new world opened up before us. I could hear Luke squeal with delight through the water, and then only the rhythmic and hollow whoosh of my own breath remained. I was immediately awestruck by the rainbow of colors in this underwater world: sea coral in shades of deep blues, pinks, and yellows met glorious fish in every size and shape imaginable who proudly showed off their bright hues and patterns. Luke and I pointed excitedly to each other and attempted to communicate through garbled snorkel talk. It was unbelievably gorgeous. How could we swim here for only an hour? Our timed sessions always seemed to end too quickly.

Squeezing his hand tightly, I kicked through the calm waters wide-eyed, joyfully observing the fish as they swam in and out of their beautiful coral abodes; they delighted us by hiding from view and then surprising us around the next corner. Each fish, large and small, was created uniquely with color combinations and markings I could have never imagined on my own. Pink, turquoise, purple, yellow, white and black with stripes, polka dots, chevron stripes, and unknown geometric patterns. Corals of every shape were appropriately named: brain, fire, and finger anemone.

We encountered stingrays, barracuda, and even several harmless reef sharks. One morning, we spotted a local sea turtle as large as a classic snow sled gliding gracefully through the reef. He infamously had only three legs because of an apparent shark incident, but his smooth strides didn't indicate that losing a limb bothered him at all. We followed him from afar and enjoyed using our underwater camera to capture his journey through his neighborhood.

Although much of the coral was pastel-hued, we did come across many sections that were dead and gray, victims of warming temperatures and environmental damage due to tourism. Back onboard our boat, a marine biologist educated us on the history of the reef and how this particular offshore outfitter was ensuring that the area they frequent was not being further damaged by human activity. But because of rising temperatures, there is concern that the habitat will continue to erode and this natural wonder of the world could one day disappear. Partly because of this, but more because we loved it so much, I am confident we will travel back to the Great Barrier Reef as soon as possible. While it may be on the opposite side of the world from our American home, this wonder captured our hearts and mesmerized our minds with its beauty. And, as Luke often reminds us, he intends to return when he is twelve so he can become scuba certified, dive deeper, and explore even more.

The final stop of our Australian itinerary was spectacular Sydney. The waterfront, with its iconic opera house and commanding harbor bridge, lived up to the hype. We spent five days exploring the city and its nearby beaches, capping off the last night by watching a fireworks show over the harbor from our hotel room. Sydney is one of the most expensive cities in the world, so we began cashing in Mitch's hard-earned hotel points for free nights of accommodation. Throughout the nine months, we would intersperse these no-cost, five-star comforts twenty-nine times.

Starwood is our preferred hotel chain and we bedded down in a gorgeous hotel on Darling Harbor. Here we enjoyed what would become our favorite splurges—king-sized beds with excellent linens and pillows, hot showers in modern bathrooms, fluffy bathrobes, and free breakfast.

Incorporating the beach and outdoors into daily living seems to be a requirement for residents of Sydney and people ferry out to the sandy shores or, if they are lucky enough, cruise on their boats through the harbor and out to the beaches beyond the city. Our budget only allowed for public transport, but we enjoyed the journey as much as the destination on the top deck of an old-fashioned ferry that carried us out to Manly Beach one sunny afternoon. Mitch and Luke braved the icy water on their boogie boards, staying out of the way of the more experienced surfers, while I watched from the shore.

Another day, we ventured to famous Bondi Beach. We paid a reasonable entry fee to swim at the famous, and aptly-named, Iceberg pool which is built into the rocks overlooking the surf. Mitch swam laps and checked off a bucket list item as the frigid ocean waves crashed over the wall onto his back. Even if you aren't a surfer or as comfortable in your swimsuit as the super-fit Australians, spending time at the beach is a quintessential Sydney pastime and we were there to immerse. Besides, I never complain about an afternoon of sun and sand.

In Sydney, we continued a newfound interest we had discovered in Melbourne—the free walking tour. It became a staple on the itinerary of almost every city we encountered. Our Aussie friends recommended the walking tour as a great way to both learn the highlights of a city and get your bearings on foot alongside a knowledgeable guide. It was quite evident that Luke learned much better from others than from our attempts at self-guided family walks. The free walking tours are led by young, smart, and engaging guides who not only kept Luke's interest, but they were also willing to engage him in conversation between stops on the tour. Indeed, it took a few tours for Luke to listen quietly and wait patiently before bombarding the guide with questions. But, with ice cream as an incentive for a successful tour, he willingly went along on more than thirty city tours all told.

These two-hour walks were an excellent way to start a trip, get the history of the city, and the lay of the land. Some we found, like the initial tour in Melbourne, even had street food stops to introduce local cuisine. The guides also provided local recommendations on restaurants and answered questions about transportation or other must-see sites. After a few months, we started inviting our guide out to lunch following the tour to share a meal and learn more about them personally. In non-English speaking countries especially, they were very eager to practice their English with us and we felt like we had gotten to know a real, local resident rather than just a tour guide. Of course, these guides work off of tips they receive from patrons at the end of the tour. We always felt it was nice to pay them what we believed they earned instead of a standard ticket price and the gratuity was money well spent.

Our stop in Sydney was not all sparkly lights and sunny beaches. We dealt with hotel construction that woke us regularly before dawn, and I spent a full day in the bed resting my back, which routinely caused me pain whenever I lifted too much weight. The multiple days of handling suitcases, however small, through Australian airports, boats, and hotels had taken its toll and I had to discipline myself to rest or risk further debilitating pain. I only mention these annoyances because our trip was not perfect. We experienced difficulties and challenges throughout the journey that reminded us we were still living a real life, a regular life, albeit in spectacular places. The world can be challenging and we had the choice to face the challenges with a positive attitude, focused on the blessings we'd been given, or dwell on the negative, which I've never found to be very healthy or helpful. Overcoming the challenges by focusing on all that was right became a family effort and I am confident that that mindset influenced our overall experience for the good. This attitude would be especially important several months later when we would have some of our lowest moments.

We completed our first month of traveling while in Sydney. It was a monumental moment as we looked back on all we had already accomplished. It was also thrilling to anticipate all that was still ahead. We had never been together as a family, day in and day out, for an entire month. That amount of free time spent one-on-one just doesn't happen for most American families. We were surprised at how quickly the days had passed and, as time does, we realized nine months would actually fly by in the blink of an eye if we weren't careful to savor and enjoy each waking moment.

TRIP TIP: Free city walking tours are our favorite way to explore a new place. Hundreds of cities have excellent tours and guides, giving you a great overview of the city. We typically do these tours on the first day at any new destination. Google "free walking tour [city]" and get to know a local while they show you their hometown.

6

Bangkok:
What's That Smell?

Our orientation to long-term travel was over and we were ready for the next, more challenging step. With a bit of anxiety about what lay ahead, we boarded our budget AirAsia flight and journeyed twelve hours to Bangkok, Thailand. This was our first visit to East Asia and the country that would be our home for the next month. We exited our taxi just after midnight and stepped onto the street that led to our hotel. There is no easing into Bangkok. The city's landscape of sensory overload hit us full force.

Pulling our bags along the broken sidewalk, we wove in and out of hawkers spinning brightly-lit flying saucers high into the black night sky above. The street vendors promised us a very good price and tried to convince Luke he needed at least three. Further along we smelled street food grilling on portable pushcarts. The chicken satay skewered on the coals would become one of Luke's dinner staples, but none of us were ever daring enough to try the crispy tarantulas or crickets sitting next to the poultry.

Just beyond the food, thirty lawn chairs were lined up and full of late-night tourists having every part of their bodies massaged. Regardless of the amazingly low prices, I knew I could never relax while reclining on a smelly street beside sweaty strangers. My exhaustion turned to a giggly hysteria as we finally reached our hotel further down the lane. What a hilarious, loud, and chaotic world we had found ourselves in!

Noise and chaos are two things I desperately try to avoid in my daily life. Everyone told us Asia would be different than anything we could have imagined, but you can't really grasp it until you walk the streets. The cacophony of the city bombards your senses. Scooters and mopeds buzz around at a furious pace, inching their way through the traffic and congregating tightly at each red light, then darting off when it turns green like a swarm of noisy hornets in a childhood cartoon. The *tuk-tuks* are a hilarious and frightening form of transportation that Luke adored and I climbed into reluctantly. What felt like nothing more than a motorized grocery cart, the colorful cabs were the easiest and cheapest form of transportation around the city. But safe, they were not. We had to relinquish our ingrained parental concern for seat belts, air bags, and even doors as we climbed into the vehicles and set off winding through the cars and invisible, often ignored, lanes on the streets and highways.

I hold one particularly dizzying experience as my most memorable *tuk-tuk* ride in Bangkok. The city streets and public spaces were awash in yellow and red flowers and bright paper bunting for the birthday celebration of the country's beloved King Adulyadej. Lights were strung along most major thoroughfares so nighttime cab journeys were like a crazy carnival ride with the wind in your face and lights streaming all around you. A huge fan of the "asphalt amusement park," Luke giggled with delight. I clutched him tightly and prayed that the journey would end without incident. When we exited, I didn't mind paying our happy driver a few extra baht to have kept us alive.

There are significant differences between the Eastern and Western parts of the world, but none surprised and confronted me more than the smell of Asia. I never fully adapted to the unusual and distinctive odor which was due to a lack of modern underground sanitation systems. It would gag me intermittently as I walked down the street. The heat was also suffocating in the crowded, urban metropolis of nearly ten million people and smells lingered longer and more pungently with rising temperatures and humidity.

On a particularly hot afternoon, we found our way to the modern, over-ground metro system for a much needed rest and air-conditioned ride across town. I was feeling overwhelmed and disappointed in myself for not being as positive and enthusiastic about this city as I had hoped. If we were going to step out of our comfort zone, I wanted to embrace it whole-heartedly and grow to love unfamiliar and uncomfortable places. I felt discouraged. Why wasn't I adapting and feeling a connection to this new city?

As I stood listlessly on the train, holding the cold metal bar as I swayed with the momentum, my eyes rested on an advertisement. The message intended to promote Turkish Airlines seemed to have been written just for me:

> *"There are those of us who like to venture to the unexplored. To see the beauty in the strange and unknown. Those of us who go out there with a sense of wonder. Bridging worlds, cultivating our curiosity, and finding delight in our differences. If you're one of us, and you want to explore more of this great planet, we're ready to take you there. It's time."*

Like a sweet wink from God, this poster spoke to me louder than all of the buzzing motorbikes below us on the street that day. What did I expect from myself on this trip? To embrace the strange and unknown. To find beauty and cultivate my curiosity (and my family's). It was a message that summed up our hopes and dreams and reminded me to be brave and confident in the plans God set before us. This journey was an answer to prayer and I had to trust and lean into that for it to be fully realized and enjoyed. My resolve was firm and my intent to seize each opportunity and embrace it wholeheartedly was steadfast from that moment on.

After the initial few days, we began to adjust to Bangkok; the kind people and their smiles were the key that unlocked my fears and anxieties in this overwhelming city. We also found the food very comforting and delicious, so we ended our short stay in the capital with a walking street food tour of Chinatown. Again, it was a blast to the senses, but we were surrounded by other friendly tourists and wonderful guides who helped us ease into authentic Asian cuisine.

After a short flight north, we settled into the smaller and more charming city of Chiang Mai. Here we found a routine of comfortable exploration of the Old Town streets still housed within crumbling walls and street food discovery that offered new and delightful delicacies every night. For less than $10 USD, we enjoyed hearty meals by sampling spicy minced pork, grilled seafood, succulent roasted chicken, and sweet mango with sticky rice. For Luke's less adventurous palate, fresh fruit smoothies and chicken satay skewers with rice sustained him for days on end.

The temporary food stalls popped up each night as the sun began to set and we delighted in walking through them. It was an education in local fare and local culture. We people watched, attempted to order and pay with grace in a foreign language and currency, and enjoyed the slower pace that was not nearly as frenetic as our previous stop. The pace would continue to ease as we visited smaller and more remote villages throughout the month of our stay.

It was mid-December, and one part of home I began missing was Christmas. Instead of seeing holiday decorations everywhere you look or hearing carols streaming from store speakers, December in Thailand was devoid of any Christmas cheer. Naturally, because it is not a holiday they celebrate. With few Christians and no adaptation of Westerners' seasonal culture, I found myself missing getting into the holiday spirit; certainly ninety-degree weather wasn't helping either.

One morning over text I lamented to my friends back home that I was missing Christmas and all the chaos that comes with it. We weren't buying presents, going to parties, or trimming a tree. It was a little sad. My wise friend Kate reminded me that Christmas need only be about the baby in a manger and me. Jesus, the reason for the season, was often forgotten in the pile of presents and chaos. Kate was experiencing the extreme opposite and had to stop and focus on what really mattered, while I was having to reflect on it since society wasn't jamming it down our throats. It was an interesting holiday paradox.

As He did many times along our journey, God sent us wonderful strangers who brought Christmas to us in that small Thai city. Our Bible Study at home, Community Bible Study, is an international organization with groups around the world. Before we left the United States, I tried to connect with several local contacts along our intended path. The first was a retired American couple living in Chiang Mai. Rich and Betsy joyfully replied to my first email as I introduced my family to them and wondered if they might suggest a local church we could visit.

"We would love to meet you all!" Rich wrote back just hours after I had reached out. "We are members of a church full of missionaries from America and other Western countries. We'd be happy to pick your family up and take you there."

The lonely piece of my heart that longed for celebrating the season was filled and overflowing as we stood in a school auditorium that Sunday morning singing traditional Christmas hymns like "O Come All Ye Faithful," "Hark the Herald Angels Sing," and my personal favorite, "Angels We Have Heard on High." Luke was even invited to join the children as they re-enacted the Nativity. He jumped right in as they wrapped him in purple cloth and a turban. He strode down the aisle holding a box portraying one of the wise men.

Rich and Betsy represented to me the love and joy that Christmas is all about. They had no idea that we were missing our community and family during this special time of year and they willingly, without question, welcomed us into their lives that day to share the joy and celebration that Christmas brings.

∾

Chiang Mai is at the foot of the northern, mountainous region of Thailand and is therefore a great jumping off spot for daily excursions for outdoor and adventure enthusiasts. We joined a zip line tour that took us an hour outside of town and into the forested hills for an afternoon in the treetops. After a short orientation, we strapped into our harnesses, buckled our helmets, and climbed into an old pickup truck. We headed off-road and up the mountain face. I felt surprisingly secure and safe, albeit holding on tightly, because we had researched the outfit thoroughly and only saw positive reviews on TripAdvisor and elsewhere online. While we were still in a somewhat under-developed country, the tourism industry thrives because of professional companies taking good care of visitors from all over the world.

Led by two local guides, we climbed onto an open platform midway up a tree, clipped onto the first cable, and prepared to soar. None of us has any fear of heights, so it was all fast and free. One by one we stepped off the ledge and rode across the sky. What exhilaration! The cool air slapped my face as I zipped past lush greenery and glimpsed the nearby mountaintops across the valley. Each ride was thirty seconds or less, but we enjoyed them more and more each time as we became comfortable sitting on nothing but canvas straps; just bouncing under the dense canopy of trees.

This excursion became symbolic of why we had come across the world and what we were hoping to experience on our journey—the excitement of new adventures and the delight of stepping off the ledge of comfort and safety to enjoy and experience the unknowns that life has to offer. It takes courage—mixed with a little bit of fear—but the reward of freedom and joy was worth immeasurably more to us than playing it safe. By letting go, we took each step into the unknown together; while we were unsure of what exactly would unfold, we knew for certain it would make each day more memorable, more exciting, and worth the effort.

TRIP TIP: When traveling to multiple countries, or if long division just isn't your forte, download the XE currency app to access every country's exchange rate right at your fingertips.

7

Elephant Nature Park:
Beautiful Beasts

During our planning phase, we knew there were a few experiences that we wanted to anchor our itinerary around, and the first of them was during the week of my forty-first birthday in Chiang Mai. After much research online, I had discovered an elephant park where volunteers could spend a week caring for the animals. This was not a resort where you trek and ride the elephants through the jungle, but rather a rescue sanctuary where volunteers pay to go and serve the animals.

"Are you sure we want to spend a whole week at this place?" Mitch was a bit skeptical about what the experience would entail, how rustic the accommodations might be, and whether all of us would be up for the challenge of working for a week around these enormous but delicate animals. "I mean, we have to *pay* to volunteer. That's not exactly budget friendly," he said.

"I know, but the reviews online are excellent and I feel like it's the right amount of working, relaxing, and stretching ourselves," I replied. "I'd like to give it a try. Consider it my birthday present," I said with a wink.

Subconsciously, Mitch and I were defining our "new" roles—his as macro transportation and logistics extraordinaire and mine as lodging and excursions expert. While we would both weigh in on all of the trip details, we found it less burdensome to divvy up the responsibilities of research and decision-making. Of course, there was always room for debate and veto power from the other. We each found comfort in leveraging our respective strengths.

As we neared our week with the elephants, I became more nervous and anxious about my "executive" decision. The rustic camp with open-air cabins, intermittent hot water, and vegetarian buffet dining might not be the experience we were looking for. While the idea of caring for elephants sounded great on paper, I wasn't sure if I would find my time well spent scooping poo for a week with other do-gooder travelers. Was I too old for this camp-like experience?

As we boarded the mini-bus on a warm Sunday morning, I looked around nervously at the other guests who were joining us, sizing them up like the first day of middle school. I wondered whether we would become friends as we worked alongside each other or if I would find them slightly annoying and have to fake a smile if they got on my nerves. I scanned the seats in front of me. There were over-eager, chatty singles. There were laid-back families with teenagers. There were young, middle-aged, and older married couples, gay and straight. It was a cornucopia of Westerners from England, France, Germany, Canada, the United States, and beyond who shared a similar vision for a vacation with purpose, a holiday with meaning. And now we were all anxious to see what the week would hold.

During the hour-long ride traveling north of Chiang Mai, we watched an introductory video about the elephants. I never knew the plight of the elephant and the centuries of torture and taming they had endured. We learned not only about the history of abuse, but that it still continues today. Elephants are trained to beg in city streets or work in forests as loggers in Southeast Asia; even perform in circuses around the world. There are sixty-six elephants at Elephant Nature Park. Many are blind from being under bright circus lights or poked with hooks while being "broken in." Some have suffered broken legs or hips from years of pulling logs, and most are mentally unstable after years of abuse.

Lek Chailert, the founder of Elephant Nature Park, dedicates her life to rescuing abused animals and bringing them home to more than 100 acres of land north of Chiang Mai. There are estimates of only 5,000 elephants remaining in all of Thailand, a decrease in half the population over the last three generations. Lek works tirelessly to find and rescue abused elephants, dogs, and cats so they can live out their days roaming freely in a peaceful, stress-free environment.

Suddenly, it didn't seem to matter whether I liked the other volunteers we were going to work with. We were all joining together for a common purpose and passion—being kind to others and giving our time and energy to animals who had been mistreated, living a life they didn't deserve. The short video brought tears to many eyes and it was just the beginning of the education we would receive throughout the week. Our common interest in volunteering bonded the group together and as we turned the corner into the lush, green valley surrounded by mountains, our eyes strained to get a first glimpse of the precious animals we would be serving for the next seven days.

And then we saw them. The elephants' large, feathery ears flapped in the warm breeze. Babies scurried between the legs of their aunties and grannies. Large trunks swung slowly. Padded feet softly pounded the dusty trails connecting the river to the fields. My eyes gazed across the vast property dotted with various shades of green and bright pink bougainvillea. They settled on the wooden house-like structure that had a welcoming wrap-around porch. Visitors leaned over the deck offering fruit to numerous elephants whose skinny tails swayed happily behind their hips. It was a Technicolor paradise, a sanctuary nestled into the hills where humans and animals seemed to reside together in peaceful harmony.

"Hello and welcome to the Elephant Nature Park."

We were greeted by three young Thai men, our volunteer coordinators (aka camp counselors). These "VCs," as they are known, would be guiding and directing us through our work days and free time, as well as answering questions, encouraging camaraderie, and organizing pick-up games of soccer before supper each night.

"We are going to break into groups. Each day you will have a morning and afternoon job," Tommy explained. "Don't worry, they won't be too hard. Just sweaty and stinky!"

We quickly learned the daily schedule which included offloading fruits and vegetables from daily delivery trucks, washing them lovingly, cutting corn and hay for food, and bedding and mucking out elephant stalls. Despite being the least glamorous task, I thought it was most fun to scoop endless shovels of poo out of elephant stalls and off the fields where they roamed. I found it hilarious and wildly refreshing that we were paying to scoop poop. It was the essence of uncomfortable, but in that service I felt a stronger bond to others around me as we helped animals who had not asked for a life of torture and were now living a deserved life of rest.

In exchange for our few hours of labor each day, we would be allowed to feed, bathe, and walk alongside the elephants under the warm sun, observing them and interacting at a safe distance. Our VCs took us on a quick tour around the property and then we got fully immersed in one of our most exciting duties . . . the river bath. Each elephant has its own *mahout*—a local Thai guide who cares for and watches over him or her. The *mahout* is especially helpful for those who are blind or lame. The *mahouts* guided four elephants to our eager group. As we held buckets, we slowly waded knee deep into the refreshingly cold water.

"Do not stand behind them or splash water in their ears," the *mahouts* gently warned. "We will keep feeding them while you wash them so they are happily distracted."

There is always order and a respectful calm when dealing with 10,000 pound creatures at Elephant Nature Park. So only when they began eating their watermelon snacks did we fill our buckets and begin splashing their rotund sides and legs.

Luke squealed with glee as he emptied his first bucket onto Maepurm, a blind and old female who had been rescued from a logging camp. With more and more enthusiasm, he quickly refilled his bucket and began unloading it faster and faster, higher and higher, until we heard screams from the other side of Maepurm. "Luke! Stop!" came the cries of our fellow volunteers. It seems they were receiving most of Luke's water onto their own heads! Thankfully most were gracious and appreciated his fun-loving attitude and unintentional shower.

After the elephant bath, we retreated to our cabin to unpack and change for supper. Our lodge held two sturdy beds wrapped in mosquito nets secured from the ceiling. The bathroom was small and felt more like an outhouse. While technically connected to our sleeping area, it had three feet of open space between the walls and roof giving a sense of showering outdoors with only a bit of privacy from our neighbors in the cabin next door.

The first night, after our supper of various vegetables, noodles, and rice, the group was taken to the upper deck of the lodge to receive a formal Thai blessing during a welcoming ceremony led by local women. Dressed in traditional robes with flowers in their hair, the women presented us with red string bracelets to wear throughout the week. Because it was my birthday, I received an Elephant Nature Park coffee table book signed by Lek herself. It is a treasure of colorful photography of all her "children"—elephants she's rescued through the years. After just one day, I knew this experience would be life changing and one of the best decisions we could have made. By going outside of our regular standards for comfort, and being open to the good intentions of this organization and what they were doing for these animals, I had received an incredible birthday gift.

"Good morning wonderful volunteers!"

The next day we were greeted early by our VCs as we queued up for the breakfast buffet of more noodles and rice.

"Group One will be working in the 'Ele Kitchen' this morning with an afternoon feeding and walk after lunch," they explained. "Group Two will be on poop-scooping duty and Group Three will ride out to the fields to gather corn stalks."

Our Group One tasks immediately became Luke's favorite chores. Pickup trucks piled high with pumpkins and watermelons needed to be unloaded and washed in the large stone trough before being sorted and delivered to the animals. Luke climbed atop the mound as the group formed a line leading from the back of the truck bed to the trough. We began a rhythmic, human conveyor belt as we passed along each dusty pumpkin toward its cold bath. Upon arrival it was met by another set of hands to wash it clean. These gourds were not like Halloween carving pumpkins, but green and yellow fruits the size of small cantaloupes. They were scrubbed and collected in buckets waiting to be distributed to hungry elephants as well as day visitors who could hand-feed the animals from the viewing porch.

Once the day's allotment was set aside, we continued our upper body workout and stacked the remaining pumpkins on an outdoor shelf for use until the next delivery. The unloading, washing, and storing of watermelons came next, but not without an accidental drop and smash every now and then. Luke was only temporarily on the watermelon crew as we quickly realized his pass-to-drop ratio was severely worse than most others. He was relegated to the wash basin. Chatting cheerfully to everyone, he never considered that as the youngest member of the group he might be any less vital to the cause.

The pace eased most afternoons as the heat intensified and we strolled through the fields with buckets and shovels to tidy the messes that were made after breakfast was digested. I enjoyed the daily routine—a life with simple, rewarding tasks surrounded by my family and new friends in a beautiful environment. One day, Lek invited us into a large meeting room with a thatched roof and bench seats. She had produced a documentary video about the plight of elephants and asked that we watch it as a group. I immediately knew it would be painful to watch, even gruesome, but we were invested in Lek's work and her cause so we watched with trepidation as the story unfolded.

When you see an elephant being ridden by humans or performing tricks for onlookers, they have been "trained" in a Phajaan ceremony. This is done to baby elephants who are taken from their mothers after just a few months. The elephant is tied in a small cage that does not allow them to move at all and is literally meant to crush his body. The baby elephant is then beaten, poked with nails, sleep-deprived, and starved for up to a week. This process is designed to purposely break their spirits so that when they are released (if they don't die in the process) they are fearful and obedient to humans. Elephants in the United States or other parts of the world more than likely have been broken in this way, too. It doesn't just happen in Asia.

As my family watched the torture of these beautiful creatures unfold, our hearts were broken. Tears and heaving gasps overtook the room as our new friends watched the horrifying plight of the animals we had grown to love. It was a necessary evil to share the video with us so that we would become advocates and spread the good work that Lek was doing. Educating friends and family not to ride elephants or support circuses with animals slowly breaks the cycle of tourism and money that perpetuates the industry of abuse; an industry that is ultimately killing the elephants off completely. Visiting this part of the world and spending time with the beautiful creatures at Elephant Nature Park inspired us to learn and educate others. Lek is changing the future for these animals and we felt blessed to be a small part of her heroic efforts.

The week seemed to fly by as we fell into a routine of communal meals and daily chores for the elephants. A blanket of sadness fell over us the following Sunday as we packed our bags and said goodbye to our new friends. Most of us were on to another destination within Thailand or Southeast Asia. Certainly we were all changed after experiencing life with the magnificent, silent, and strong creatures.

TRIP TIP: Elephant Nature Park offers day trips and overnight excursions for visitors seeking to experience the beauty of Thailand and its national mascot. Lek and her team have built a worthwhile and hands-on experience for families with kids of all ages to see and touch the rescued creatures. There is no riding, but visitors can feed, bathe, and pet the animals. We highly recommend investing in a week of volunteer work.

8

Koh Yao Noi: When I'm Missing, You'll Find Me Here

We celebrated Christmas at an international resort in Phuket. It was the first time that our family had swapped a decorated Christmas tree and stockings hanging by the roaring fireplace for fireworks and warm days at the beach. After working hard at Elephant Nature Park, we enjoyed our days relaxing and swimming in the sea. At night after watching the sun set behind the palm trees, we summoned Christmas traditions by reading the Nativity story and "The Night Before Christmas." On Christmas Eve, Santa Claus cleverly managed to find Luke in room 677 and gifted him with three small toys that would easily fit in his backpack as we continued traveling.

When it was time to host our first family visitor we destined for the smaller Thai island of Koh Yao Noi. It is the northernmost island in the Andaman Sea, worlds away from the more hectic and tourist beaches of Phuket and Krabi. Mitch's brother, Walker, flew across the world to spend the week between Christmas and New Years with us. We inhabited a spot that was most "on the ledge" and out of our comfort zone, and Koh Yao Noi became a wonderful escape from any world we had ever known. When I reflect on our trip, our adventures in Thailand often come to mind. It was the furthest from what any of us had ever experienced before and the exquisiteness of the landscape and people romantically drew me in.

Koh Yao Noi is a fairly quiet and uninhabited island so we opted for ultra rustic accommodations: renting a treehouse bungalow with a thatched roof and hammocks, mosquito nets, and intermittent running water. The balmy, warm air blew through the open windows and tiny green tree frogs hopped in and out of the bungalow as we unloaded our bags and changed permanently into our bathing suits.

On the path just outside our door, we were greeted by what became our unofficial mascot—a large monitor lizard who alternatively sped or lazily crawled through the brush around and underneath our bungalow. We named him "Monty" and he reminded me of a pet dog. While I wasn't brave enough to pet the scaly beast that probably weighed in around forty pounds, he was practically tame. We would often find him basking in the rays of sunlight slicing through the palm trees or sneakily rustling through the garbage outside the resort's kitchen. I'll admit though, after meeting Monty I began making extra noise whenever we were walking back to our hut so as not to accidently step on him or meet him face to face on our front porch.

We split our time between lazily swinging in beachside hammocks and exploring the smaller islands. It was refreshing and fun to kayak into caves, hike cliffs, and bicycle around our new temporary island home. What I expected to be a busy island filled with vacationers was more of a quiet secret and we reveled in the fact that not many tourists had discovered our hideaway. We had the white sand beaches to ourselves, rising early to watch the sunrise. Seeing it set again over the dramatic rock karsts in the sea made for beautiful bookends to the long days that left us salty and sunburned.

One of my favorite excursions began early one morning when we were met at the water's edge by a long-tail boat and our guide for the day, Mi. The five of us waded out to the old but sturdy wooden boat and climbed aboard for a day of sightseeing and island hopping. Our first stop was a shaded cove surrounded on almost all sides by towering rock karsts. The cliffs shot out of the aquamarine water and hovered above us as we untied the sea kayaks secured to our boat's roof and laid them gently in the water. Slowly we paddled in and out of the towering formations and slid into the caves and tunnels the water had created. Though only mid-morning, the sun shone brightly and we enjoyed splashing each other with our oars to cool off.

"Would you like to visit Bat Island next?" Mi inquired as we climbed back into the boat and refreshed our throats with ice cold Coca-Colas.

"Sure! That sounds fun!" my ever-enthusiastic Luke responded.

Hmmm. *Why is it called Bat Island?* I thought fleetingly as the motor started and we headed out. Much to my dismay, it was a simple and very literal naming that shook me to my very core.

I'm not a fan of bats although I know and appreciate the fact that they eat mosquitos, my summer nemesis. The rest of my familial companions did not seem timid as we pulled alongside a deserted shoreline and hopped out into a mangrove forest. After walking only a few yards, I began hearing an eerie screeching sound, but it wasn't until we were fully immersed in the forest that Mi told us to look up. Literally *thousands* of bats the size of watermelons were hanging upside down, blanketing the trees with such density that it was difficult to see the sky beyond them. I almost fainted with fright.

"Oh dear Lord!" I gasped. "I have got to get out of here!"

The boys thought I was exaggerating and were intrigued by all of the hovering "blood-suckers," but I was not sticking around to see if the bats would welcome us or not. I turned and bolted back to the beach. I was shivering uncontrollably and only caught my breath once I was back on board our boat. What seemed like an innocent nature viewing had thoroughly creeped me out! Our next stop was much less dramatic. Visiting a 700-year-old enormous banyan tree and having a picnic lunch on the sand was more my speed.

Each island had its own charm and was just as deserted as the first. We rode for hours across the crystal clear water, soaking up the warm sun and marveling at the beautiful land formations that make Thailand famous. The memories are visceral. I can still taste the salt air and feel the gentle bounce of the long-tail that we cruised on well into the evening. If I ever disappear, you should probably start by looking for me there.

On New Year's Eve, we loaded into the back of a pickup truck owned by one of the local seaside restauranteurs. He had recently opened another dinner spot at the top of a nearby mountain and we decided it was the perfect place to ring in the New Year. We arrived in time to see the sun set over the water, painting pastels across the sky. The tiny cumulus clouds were backlit pink and blue as we bid the year farewell and then the sun disappeared behind another mountaintop. The other guests had apparently only come for the sunset so we found ourselves to be the only guests staying through dinner. We ordered a plethora of dishes to sample and suddenly, we became VIPs. The cocktails kept arriving and the owner became our personal DJ. As it neared midnight, we became fast friends with the entire extended family who were all pitching in to cook, serve, and host. We all danced into the night until fireworks lit up the sky and reflected brightly over the sea. It was an incredible way to usher in a new year full of adventures.

As we returned to Bangkok for our last few days in Thailand, I pondered all we had undertaken in just two months and the potential for new experiences in the year ahead. It was such an education: seeing the diverse regions of this beautiful country, getting over the smells, embracing the lack of modernity, sampling new foods, meeting extraordinarily kind people, and serving gentle animals. The memories and experiences in Thailand will forever be treasured by our family.

How was it possible to love each place we visited more than the one before? Surely we would not continue on this spellbinding path beyond Thailand? Something would inevitably slow us down, abruptly change our course, or throw us for a loop. We were certainly prepared for obstacles, but as of yet there had been none.

Or, had there been? Maybe we were confidently choosing to be positive and that set the tone for taking on each new day as an adventure despite some obstacles. What a freeing feeling to know that each day was so unknown to us, monotony was dead, and there were no expectations or routines to adhere to. I was learning to adapt and not let fear and unfamiliarity rule my consciousness. Experiencing the new and different was refreshing for my soul and reinvigorated my senses, sometimes to the point of exhaustion.

While some may find it unsettling to stretch beyond the artificial guardrails that keep us on course, somehow our family was wholeheartedly embracing it. I continued to think deeply about the lessons I was learning along the way and they continued to point back to trusting God. I had to rely on Him and trust that He was guiding and directing us. There was less anxiety and more peace in our hearts with each day that passed. This inner peace diminished our fears and apprehension and gave us the wild-hearted courage to continue.

We said goodbye to Mitch's brother and thanked him for crossing the globe to see us. We also took advantage of the opportunity to send some unnecessary baggage back home with Walker. We started the trip with a small amount of luggage and even still found that we did not need all of it. We filled an entire duffle bag with extra shirts, pants, and a few souvenirs to keep our bags light.

Before leaving home, I had gleefully anticipated living simply; letting go of my vanity—going make-up and hair product-free with just a few choices of clothing. And, after just two months, we learned we needed even less than we had packed. What does that say about our reliance on material things? As we stripped our "stuff" away, we could focus more on each other and the experiences we were having together. Plus, the lighter suitcases made my back happy.

Instead of being dependent on my "things," I was learning to be more dependent on God. Our family was stretching, sometimes painfully, as we grew together. Spending 100 percent of each day and night together can be challenging for a family. It requires a selfless heart and I constantly needed to go beyond myself for patience and unconditional love. Sadly, I sometimes struggled to get through a day without making a snide comment, rolling my eyes, or heaving a frustrated sigh, but my greatest desire was for family harmony. I was learning so much about the depths of grace and love—not just what I could offer—but what God was willing to fill me with, when I stayed open to opportunities. I realized He was the travel necessity I could not live without.

TRIP TIP: Baby free! Especially in Southeast Asia, but all over the world, kids are beloved. And for many activities, transportation, and meals, they are free. Don't be afraid to ask, "Baby free?" For kids under twelve, you'll enjoy a discount more often than not.

9

Cambodia:
Adding to the Itinerary

When we were plotting out our travel path, we definitely agreed on visiting Thailand and Vietnam. So when I picked up a travel book to research Southeast Asia, I was surprised to find one of the top sites in the world sitting right between those two countries. We had never considered stopping in Cambodia. I knew very little about the country except that Angelina Jolie adopted her first son there after filming *Tomb Raider*. The iconic ruins caught my eye and I decided we would be crazy to miss Siem Reap, Cambodia, and the temples of Angkor.

Each day, Asia found some way to nudge me out of my comfort zone and I learned to expect and even appreciate the unknown. Our departure from Thailand meant a nine-hour, overland journey by bus into Cambodia. Mitch had researched the route diligently, but it was a nerve-racking trek. To keep within our budget, it made the most sense to *drive* rather than *fly*. What did not make sense was actually boarding the bus, walking across the border, finding another bus, and then finally hailing a taxi which would take us eventually to our destination—all in a third world country with which I wasn't familiar.

Sometimes I let my imagination get the best of me and I had to suppress it as we climbed aboard a pre-paid mini-bus with six other Western tourists that humid morning in early January. We had already maxed out our thirty-day travel visa in Thailand and it was time to depart; and even though we booked the transportation through our hotel, I was really anxious about the journey. We crept slowly through the web of Bangkok traffic and after a few hours traded skyscrapers for flat, deserted fields and endless, dusty highways. I put in my earbuds to drown out our traveling companions' snoring and tried to focus on anything but the idea of being abducted and held for ransom by the sleazy-looking driver.

Our "lunch stop" options consisted of a roadside gas station mini mart and a street food shack that even the most adventurous eater would avoid. We huddled outside the mini mart under a sliver of shade the building offered and I continued praying that we would make it to the border alive. I had booked a large, air-conditioned room at what looked to be a quaint and clean boutique hotel in Siem Reap and as the hours rolled on I just focused on getting our family there in one piece.

As we neared the border of Cambodia, we were asked to exit the bus with our luggage. We were forewarned that this was a normal part of the process, but I still had an uneasy feeling that we would be left on the side of the road for dead. There was some comfort in numbers. Alongside other weary and weathered backpackers, we dragged our bags into the Thai immigration office where we were stamped out of the country.

Now literally in "no-man's land," pedestrians, belching trucks, motorcyclists, and semis collectively waited to cross through the border gates. We stopped for a brief selfie in front of the "Welcome to Cambodia" archway and then proceeded to walk another 100 yards to the office where officials would process our Cambodian travel visas. With $75 USD cash in our pockets (thanks Walker!), we filled out the paperwork, paid, and received our next stamp and visa. I was beginning to feel my load lighten when I realized we still had to connect with our chauffeur on the other side. We bid farewell to one minibus but I had no idea where to find the next one that would take us the rest of the way.

It was during these steps across the border that I remembered we were not the only travelers in the world. If the three of us had been the only Westerners at this border stop, I would have been out of my mind with fear and anxiety. But there were at least twenty others in our group, so we shuffled slowly alongside them, glancing to each other, and smiling apprehensively as if to say, "We're in this together, right?"

After what seemed like an eternity of standing in the blazing heat, we found our bus and climbed aboard. The driver then promised us—in broken English—that he was taking us to the final rendezvous. There, in a random parking lot, we were cheerfully greeted by two Cambodian men who couldn't have been more than twenty years old.

"Hello! We take you to Siem Reap!"

They pointed to a 1980's Toyota Camry. Mitch and I exchanged glances, shrugged our shoulders, and jammed our family of three into the backseat with backpacks in our laps.

Two hours later, we rolled into Siem Reap and were welcomed by our gracious hosts at The Villa Hotel. Ice cold A/C, fresh fruit juice, and chilled hand towels were offered as we arrived from our journey. We had survived! And all three of us felt we had accomplished something much greater in nine hours than driving just 250 miles.

As we lounged by the refreshingly cold pool at the hotel that afternoon, I realized that the best memories are made when we push ourselves and do something that seems—to us—very unnatural. The easy, comfortable, and routine does not a memory make. I could have easily paid the $200 USD and gotten on an airplane for an hour, but that day's experience was one we would never forget. Who doesn't want to ride into Cambodia with two guys in a Camry pointing out rice fields and offering great food recommendations? It was a trip. Literally. We tried to keep smiling despite our concerns and fears. But that is part of why we invested in the journey in the first place—to get out of our comfort zone, onto the ledge, and face the fear of the unknown.

Siem Reap reminded me of a dusty, old Mexican town and we quickly fell in love with our little neighborhood. Next door to our hotel was My Little Café where we ate fresh, delicious meals literally every day. The café served excellent (and cheap!) Cambodian, Thai, and even a bit of American food that satisfied all of us for less than $10 USD total. Surprisingly, the Cambodian currency was U.S. dollars, having more stability in economic markets than the Cambodian Riel. We marveled every time we visited an ATM and saw American dollars spit out.

We started our days with fresh fruit smoothies and Luke would inevitably get a ham and cheese sandwich. Mitch discovered his favorite Cambodian specialty dish was fish *amok*, a thick broth with spicy heat and chunks of fresh white fish and vegetables. *Amok* is similar to a curry but flavored with cinnamon and served in a hand-crafted banana leaf bowl. When I wasn't ordering my go-to Thai dish of *pad med mamuang* (cashew nut chicken), I tested my palate with more traditional Cambodian dishes like *lok lak* (a stir fry with beef or chicken and vegetables), banana flower salad, and fresh spring rolls.

We explored the town of Siem Reap, which was a bit overrun by backpackers, and anticipated our first glimpse of Angkor Wat the next day. A three-day pass would give us ample time over our weeklong stay to explore the temples and ruins across the 100,000-acre site.

We took advice from a travel blogger and hired a *tuk-tuk* driver for our first day of exploring the temples. Marom was a reputable old man who guided us through the entry gates and down the long and dusty road leading from Siem Reap to Angkor. We passed local schools full of tanned children who smiled widely and waved to us in our open-air cart as they played in the dirt outside the cinderblock building, and we narrowly missed being attacked by a pack of monkeys desperate for tourist snacks.

Angkor was the ancient capital city of the Khmer Empire and flourished from the ninth to eleventh centuries with more than one million residents at a time when London had just 50,000, making it the largest city in the world prior to the Industrial Revolution. Angkor was built as a temple complex to the Hindu gods and each structure is an architectural wonder. Five million massive sandstones were ferried from a quarry more than thirty miles upstream. An estimated 300,000 workers and 6,000 elephants (much to my dismay) constructed the complex. While some ruins are now overgrown by nature and the jungle, painstaking restoration and reconstruction now means millions of visitors can again visit what *Lonely Planet* deemed the number one wonder of the world.

Marom recommended we start small so we could build to a grand finale on day three of our visit. He dropped us off at Preah Khan, a maze of corridors and doorways that shrunk as you moved out further from the center. This was Luke's first revelation that the temples of Angkor were the inspiration for one of his favorite video games, Temple Run.

Mitch cleverly suggested Luke should imitate the animated monkeys running through narrow, rocky pathways and they spent the afternoon making videos. They turned our history lessons into real-life re-enactments to be shared later with his friends back home.

We found the best way to engage Luke in historical sights and museums was to keep our expectations realistic for an eight-year-old's interest level. Sometimes that meant creatively exploring a place instead of reading every sign posting or shortening our visit to only the highlights. We wanted Luke to be excited about learning, so Mitch and I were willing to gauge our child's interest level and finish on a high note instead of dragging him around longer than his attention span allowed.

The famed Ta Prohm was next on our list and we walked and climbed amongst the ruins where massive trees have suffocated the collapsing temple. Nature proved stronger than man as the roots thicker than my torso pushed through blocks of stone and were, in some cases, the cement that kept the temple walls intact.

"Dad, video me!" Luke's game became his favorite way to explore each temple.

"I'm going to fall and break my ankle," Mitch lamented to me with a smile as he and Luke set up their course and delicately maneuvered around the wobbling stones.

I walked quietly in the opposite direction, half hoping not to be associated with my monkeys running through the sacred grounds, but also to lose myself in the quiet maze of hallways and rooms now open to the sky. The mystical etchings inside the thick, cold extensive corridors set in an environment of gigantic trees made this an ancient playground for curious and playful visitors alike. It was unreal.

The morning after our day with Marom, we decided to rent bicycles and tour the property on our own. Now that we were a bit more familiar with the layout of the grounds, we were able to navigate to some of the lesser-known sites, climbing steep steps to vast jungle vistas and peeking into dark, abandoned tunnels. I found the mystery of the once-glorious, then-forgotten, and now reimagined temples much more interesting in their stripped down and crumbling state than the shiny, sparkling, and sterile temples of Thailand.

Early one morning, we ventured out of our hotel and caught a *tuk-tuk* to see the sunrise over Angkor Wat, the centerpiece of all the temples and the largest religious site in all of the world. We were met by thousands of other pilgrims who were also hoping to capture this moment. We all waited in the dark. As the sun came up behind the temple, a hazy, golden halo encircled the pointed silhouette. The crowd hushed as we gazed upon the beautiful site. I imagine for some it was a deeply religious experience, but for us it was simply a marvel—an awe-inspiring lesson in archaeology, architecture, and cultural history. For Cambodians, Angkor Wat and its rebirth serves as a source of inspiration and pride as they struggle to rebuild their lives after years of terror and trauma.

Just a few decades ago, Cambodia experienced tyranny and

unfathomable bloodshed. As I would learn in other countries along our journey, I was embarrassingly naïve and ignorant about Asia's turbulent history, even though I was thriving in another country on this same planet at the same time.

The Khmer Rouge, followers of the Communist Party of Kampuchea in Cambodia, was formed in 1968 as an offshoot of the Vietnam People's Army from North Vietnam. Allied with communist regimes during the Vietnam War and led by Pol Pot, the Khmer Rouge orchestrated a Cambodian genocide over four long years, killing more than two million citizens in an effort to cleanse the country of intellectuals and re-establish a more agricultural society. More than a quarter of the country was wiped out and the dark period in their history is known as the Killing Fields.

I continued challenging myself to read a book set in each country we visited. One that stayed with me long after I finished reading it was a true story of a young girl who survived the Killing Fields genocide and later moved to America. *When Broken Glass Floats*[2] is a moving recounting of the atrocities told from the heart of a little girl. The genuine rawness and truth transported me back to that time and place. The story is still fresh and painful since survivors are only now rebuilding their lives in Siem Reap and all of Cambodia.

We had the pleasure of visiting a silk and artisan's workshop which was started as an effort to give displaced people new skills and jobs. Their craftsmanship was exquisite and as we walked through the factory's rooms, we witnessed lives rebuilt and stories told through woodworking, metalworking, and silk art. In our tour group, a woman was researching a book she was penning about her own husband's experience and survival. To spend time with people who had experienced such unimaginable tragedy and see them flourishing on the other side was deeply touching.

The Cambodian display of strength of the human spirit and the sheer will of survival inspired me. Knowing that our futures do

---

[2] Chanrithy Him, When Broken Glass Floats (W.W. Norton & Company, 2000.)

not have to be defined by our past and that good things can come after a seemingly endless period of darkness encourages me in such a rapidly changing world.

TRIP TIP: If you are traveling often or for an extended period of time internationally, research a bank that doesn't charge ATM fees for using third-party banks, such as a Charles Schwab checking account. It's always smart to have a second account as a back-up for getting cash. Store the extra ATM card in a safe place, not in your wallet.

10

Vietnam:
Our Biggest Surprise

After a week in Cambodia, we were feeling confident and ready for our next Southeast Asian stop, Vietnam. I timidly agreed to put Vietnam on our itinerary because it was one of Mitch's top requests. His father fought in the Vietnam War as a Naval Officer, so it was important for Mitch to visit.

Having only learned about Vietnam from America's point of view, I was concerned that we would not be welcome in a country where we had done so much damage. I was a bit apologetic and embarrassed that we were American, not because I approved of Communism, but because we played a part in so many lives being lost—both ours and theirs.

We had three weeks to spend in the country, but since we aimed to travel slow Mitch and I weighed the pros and cons of which city to see, either Hanoi in the north or Ho Chi Minh City in the south. We ultimately decided on Hanoi because of its smaller size, colonial French influence, and proximity to Halong Bay, another bucket list destination for us. After reading of its character and charm, Mitch proposed that we start in Hoi An, a small coastal town in the center of the long and skinny country. I'm so glad he was enthusiastic about Vietnam and researched this ancient port town because it became my favorite spot in the country.

Hoi An was a French colonial town in the seventeenth and

eighteenth centuries known for its trading port and midway position between the northern and southern ends of the country. Largely undamaged by the Vietnam War, the yellow two- and three-story buildings that make up the pedestrianized Old Town have the worn charm of villages in the South of France today. Still a port of commerce and trade, as a tourist you can see authentic Vietnamese life happening at the waterside open market and in the many haberdasheries where a tailored suit can be custom made for a fraction of what it would cost in the United States.

We booked a room at a homestay—the Vietnamese version of a bed and breakfast—with a precious family of three generations. This homestay offered five spacious and modern rooms and an outdoor courtyard for serving breakfast. They immediately took us in, asking if we would join them and the other guests for a family-style dinner. It was a delicious feast of noodles, beef, spring rolls, and cakes for dessert. We fell in love with their hospitality and warmth, and I was quickly won over and convinced that most Vietnamese had long since moved on from the negative feelings they may have once harbored for Americans.

"They've got free bikes, Mom!" Luke exclaimed after breakfast our first morning. "Let's ride out to the beach!"

"I read Anthony Bourdain found some delicious *banh mi* sandwiches in the Old Town. Maybe we could get lunch there?" Mitch added. Food and freewheeling. Our day's plans were firmed up by 8:00 a.m.

Our favorite family activities were slowly formulating as we ventured into each new town and discovered things all three of us could enjoy together. One delightful surprise was our love of discovering a new city via bicycle. Luke impressed us with his willingness to adapt to any size and style bike, and we found we could cover much more ground on two *wheels* instead of two *feet*.

Our intention was to purposefully spend time together soaking up what life was like around the world. We wanted to peel away the layers of schedules and busyness that enveloped our family and spend weeks at a time in different places where we knew only each other. At home, it was sometimes hard to slow down and find time to play a simple board game or take a bike ride as a family. Old fashioned family activities seemed to be drowned out by baseball, basketball, Cub Scouts, swim practice, and of course, TV. But on our journey, simple was all we had. Seeking out a bicycle rental outfit in almost every city we visited became a treasured part of our routine, spending hours riding side by side as we explored.

Another surprise delight was investing in cooking courses to learn the country's cuisine. In Thailand and Cambodia, we had taken cooking classes and we wanted to do the same in Vietnam. We found that the key to our hearts was through our stomachs when arriving in a new destination. There seemed to be no better way to make the unfamiliar look appetizing than to chop, stir, and cook it ourselves.

Each cooking guide takes the group to the local market for fresh ingredients, a great lesson in the local fare. This was Luke's least favorite part because of the inevitable stinky fish and seafood purveyors, but I loved perusing the stalls and gazing over the brightly-colored fruits and vegetables. Later, back in the classroom kitchen, we each chose the dish we wanted to make from a selection of options and set up our ingredients at a cooking station. Traditional dishes that may have been intimidating on a menu now looked, smelled, and tasted delicious. Luke has always been a picky eater, preferring simple and uncomplicated meals where no two items touch on the plate. But the process of shopping, chopping, and the new responsibilities of cooking over his own stovetop miraculously opened his mind and palate to the local cuisine.

Our excursion to Thuan Tinh Island Cooking School in Hoi An was undoubtedly my favorite cooking experience of the entire trip. We met Trang, our young and eager guide/interpreter, at the waterside market one drizzly afternoon. We walked the aisles alongside women and men of all ages and she introduced us to a few unfamiliar vegetables, fruits, and herbs. Then we carried our burgeoning shopping bags aboard a river boat which had been waiting to take us up the waterway through the mangroves.

An hour later, we arrived at a remote, thatched bungalow; our beautiful setting for the next three hours of cooking. Ti, our instructor, welcomed us with a wide smile as we climbed off the boat and carried our raw ingredients from the dock. She reminded me of a Vietnamese version of my grandmother, her white apron pulled tight across her ample figure. Ti's strong arms guided us to the bungalow and all the while she was talking ninety miles an hour in Vietnamese. With the help of Trang's English instruction and service of endless glasses of fresh passionfruit juice, Ti guided us over our woks as we created four quintessential Vietnamese dishes.

Our first course was *banh xeo*, delicate and savory Vietnamese crepes filled with pork and shrimp, bean sprouts, and green onion. The *bun bo nam bo* was fresh and tangy, an herb salad with rice vermicelli and sautéed beef, topped with roasted peanuts and hot soy sauce vinaigrette. While the first two courses were completely new to me, the final two were Vietnamese staples I had tried before. *Pho bo*—perfect for our rainy afternoon—is a beef noodle soup infused with beef bones, cinnamon, ginger, and star anise; a gorgeous, clear, but flavorful, soup that warmed me from the inside out. Finally, we mastered fresh spring rolls. These wraps were similar to the ones we had made in Thailand—filled with fresh herbs, pork, shrimp, and a decadent peanut hoisin dipping sauce.

The very fact we could cook and enjoy these dishes laced with peanuts is a little miracle in itself. Luke was born with a severe nut allergy and could have kept us from going on our trip around the world. The anxiety over interpreting foreign menus and translating with cooks and waiters was a big concern for me, especially in the Southeast Asian countries where nuts are so prevalent in many of their signature dishes. Luke had been diagnosed at only eighteen months old with his allergy that included not only peanuts, but sesame seeds, cashews, and most other tree nuts. Through the years we diligently carried an Epi-Pen and he was labeled a "nut-free" kid, but thankfully he never faced any of the life-threatening reactions that many children of his generation experience.

When we were planning our trip, it struck me that we needed to know exactly how allergic to nuts Luke was. I wanted to be as prepared as possible if something were to slip into his meal. After years of precautionary measures, we found ourselves sitting in the doctor's office one morning with a bag of peanut M&M's.

"We'll start with just one," the pediatric allergist explained as we opened the yellow bag. "If we see a reaction, we have nurses on hand with Benadryl or an Epi-Pen to handle any emergencies."

Really? This is how we are going to test the strength of his allergy? I thought. We had done skin and blood tests before, but the rubber was really hitting the road this morning as we eyed the first red candy being consumed.

"How do you feel?" I asked Luke tentatively. "Is your throat itchy?"

"Nope. It tastes really good!" he responded. "Can I have another?"

"Not for twenty minutes," the doctor replied. "I'll be back then, but come get us in the meantime if anything changes."

Well, nothing happened. So after twenty minutes Luke got to eat two M&M's. And, after what felt like the longest morning ever in a doctor's office, he managed to eat the entire bag of candy without a single concern. The numerous, idling hours were not wasted, though. We learned his allergy, however severe it had been as a toddler, was now minimal and non-life threatening. This was amazing news as we headed east to foreign menus and unfamiliar dishes. I still thought it best to travel with *four* Epi-Pens, but we were much less concerned about the chance of an international hospital visit and could enjoy trying new things without the fear of anaphylactic shock.

Our afternoon at the cooking school reinforced my growing fondness for the Vietnamese people. We were finding their hospitality very warm and inviting. There was no pushy or overbearing sentiment as we interacted, and I never felt any animosity toward us as Americans. It seemed the younger generation of Vietnamese were thrilled to connect with Westerners and the older generation was kind and forgiving—as if what happened forty years ago was truly in the past.

These rich experiences replicated themselves again and again as we moved north toward Hanoi. A student group called Hanoi Kids offers free walking tours and we found the city ambassadors delightfully engaging as they practiced their English and quizzed us about life in America.

"Do you want to be my Facebook friend?" Mai asked shyly as we walked. "We have Facebook now!"

The young generation was eager to discuss politics, social media, education, and dreams of an international career. Their enthusiasm for their home country wasn't diminished, but they embraced the trends and opportunities the modern world held.

In Hue, a significant, historic city bombed by Americans during the war, our local, English-speaking guide was adorable. Thu was a young entrepreneurial woman who had just started her own walking tour company. After a thorough tour of the significant sights, my favorite stop was to her local neighborhood bakery. There we met the third-generation baker and tried delicacies reminiscent of the French colonists' from more than a hundred years ago. These sweet and savory experiences brought us more insight and pleasure into the Vietnamese people and culture than any monument or historic sight ever could.

An arctic blast from Southern China arrived in Hanoi and we quickly found that our "chasing summer" wardrobe was woefully insufficient. Thankfully, a short walk from our Airbnb apartment to the Old Town revealed street after street of North Face winter wear for a fraction of the American price. Whether they were knockoffs or authentic, we didn't care. For $25 USD each, we gratefully purchased puffy winter coats to layer over our thin t-shirts and summer jackets.

Despite Hanoi's cold and dreary weather that week, we took

to the city. Mitch visited Hoa Lo Prison, nicknamed the Hanoi Hilton, and several other war museums to honor his father's service. We explored bicycle routes around Ho Tay Lake and attended a traditional water puppet show at a theater in the historic Hoan Kiem lake district.

Hanoi's traffic is not for the faint of heart and one morning our tour guide Li, who was leading us on a street food tour through the Old Town, stopped the group at the edge of the sidewalk.

"Dis is where we cross the road," she explained. "I need you all to be like sticky rice. Stay together and we cross slowly. Da cars will come, but you stick wit me and we make it across."

Our fellow tourists glanced nervously at us and Luke grabbed my arm tightly. Without a crosswalk or even a traffic signal to slow or stop traffic, six lanes of vehicles were flowing at a continuous pace with no intention of stopping. Li stepped into the road, and we timidly followed.

"Sticky rice, sticky rice," she chirped over and over as we inched forward.

Miraculously, as if our group was an overturned magnet repelling the cars' metal, the automobiles, *tuk-tuks,* and mopeds weaved around us and continued on. We shuffled slowly past the whizzing traffic and arrived safely on the other side.

"Very good," Li lauded. "See, sticky rice keep us together and no one get squashed."

My parental instincts battled my body every time we crossed the road in Hanoi, but our nerves had steeled after six weeks in Asia and we found our "sticky rice" moments to be a hilarious and death-defying game of chicken.

The winter weather seemed to hang over the northern section of the country and our first attempt for an excursion into Halong Bay on an overnight junk boat was delayed because of rain. We had received great recommendations about Tam Coc National Park, a few hours south of Hanoi, so we made a hasty reservation over the phone at a new resort based on the owner's promise of heat and lovely accommodations.

When we arrived, we quickly realized the heating they offered would not warm us from the forty-degree temperatures. The bungalows, while brand new and beautiful, had open air windows and the frigid air was seeping through the bamboo walls. I was so disappointed because the landscape was positively stunning. Rocky cliffs dramatically dropped into the valleys and waterways below. We had envisioned riding bikes through the countryside and hiking in the hills, but instead we huddled around a single space heater and bundled up in literally every stitch of clothing from our suitcases—layer upon flimsy layer.

Despite the colder temperatures and disappointing weather at the end, we count Vietnam as one of our favorite, most treasured countries. The laughter that came out of us as we bundled together under the duvet was much more memorable than a perfect, warm night in the rural countryside.

Thankfully we were able to visit Halong Bay on our second attempt. We cruised through rock karst islands with twenty other guests on a traditional, wooden junk boat exploring pearl farms, sea kayaking through caves, and feasting on traditional delicacies. The fog and drizzle added a romantic and mysterious air to the famous waterways and we ended our visit to Vietnam with a beautiful experience that no amount of cold weather could take away.

TRIP TIP: Don't be afraid of street food. Whether or not you are on a budget, you will want to taste the local flavor of a city. Try the food from local markets and street food vendors. Mitch enjoyed a homemade banh mi with egg each morning which he purchased from a kind woman outside our apartment. After our Hanoi street food walking tour, we returned again and again to the recommended local spots that were some of the tastiest, most authentic in town.

11

Hong Kong:
Happy New Year!

When Luke was born, Mitch and I made the decision that I would stay home with our baby full time. It was a sacrifice, but one I happily adjusted to, wanting to spend that time caring for him while he was young and enjoying each day as he grew and developed into a young boy.

I went back to work when Luke started pre-school, and now five years had passed since he and I spent long days together, every moment in sync day after day. The adage is true—the days are long but the years fly by. Preschool, then elementary school took him away for longer stretches at a time. He grew more independent each year, and we spent less time together.

As I looked at him gazing out the airplane window the morning we departed Vietnam en route to Hong Kong, I saw an amazing transformation taking place. Our son, who had always been positive and energetic, was simply thriving through our adventure. My fears and concerns over whether he would understand, enjoy, or have the stamina for our pace of travel had washed away. I saw his little mind absorbing so much, and I was so thankful that God had placed in his DNA the same love of travel that Mitch and I had. Our time together was rich, and I had to remind myself of that when the long hours wore on me. It was not always blissful, our little party of three. But after three months together 24/7, we still loved one another and were sincerely enjoying it, never regretting the decision to climb aboard the wild ride on which we had embarked.

The woman who first inspired us to travel around the world was waiting for us in Hong Kong. Selma had returned from her journey and re-settled in her hometown. She welcomed us with fervor and toured us through the historic and vibrant city as its residents bustled around in the days leading up to Chinese New Year. The "year of the monkey" was upon us and, thanks to Mitch's strategic planning, we were seeing Hong Kong at its most celebrated time. Chinese New Year added excitement and energy to our visit, but I imagined the city was always full of color and light. The skylines were more impressive than any metropolis I'd ever seen, and the views during the day rivaled the dramatic neon-lit skyscrapers that danced at night. With a harbor in between the two shorelines, you could enjoy the view wherever you stood.

"We like to thank the mainlanders for these bright blue skies," Selma explained, with a hint of sarcasm. "Because of the holidays, all of the Chinese factories are shut down and we can enjoy a few weeks of smog-free air."

Indeed, the gray and dreary skies had vanished and Hong Kong's air was crisp and clean.

We always appreciate seeing a city through the eyes of a local, and Selma took us to every nook and cranny introducing us to the food, culture, quirks, and history of Hong Kong. The waterway that divides the massive city of skyscrapers provides a passageway for ships and ferries to shuttle its residents and visitors seamlessly from side to side. She began our tour on the Kowloon side of mainland China with a walk down Birdcage Alley and the Flower Market. Bustling as people bought bouquets for their family and friends hosting New Year's celebrations, we learned the special, long-held customs that reminded me of our Christmas traditions at home.

"During the New Year's holiday," Selma explained, "we are quite busy visiting family for several days in a row."

"The younger generation—my age," she continued, "is expected to arrive at our grandparents' home with a bouquet of fresh flowers. In return, we have red envelopes filled with money waiting for us."

As we strolled through the markets, we saw kiosks full of the aforementioned red and gold envelopes embossed with traditional Chinese characters signifying love, luck, and happiness. As the days progressed, just like our shopping aisles back home, the shelves became sparse and emptied of all the gifts just in time for the exchanges to ensue.

At lunchtime, we followed Selma up an old staircase off a quiet side street and emerged into a packed dining room with bright red carpet and large, round tables set formally with white tablecloths and silverware. We were about to experience our first traditional dim sum lunch. As we entered the room and followed the maitre d' across the floor, all eyes slowly followed Mitch's tall frame—we were the only white-skinned Westerners in the place, and they were slightly stunned. Selma led us confidently to our seats across from two women already perusing the menu.

"This is my favorite dim sum restaurant in the city," she said. "I would love to order for us and allow you to try many of the signature dishes."

"You lead the way!" Mitch exclaimed. We love nothing better than following someone in the know, so Selma showed us her choices as she marked them with a pencil on the paper sheet, much like if we ordered sushi in a restaurant at home.

The dishes arrived sporadically and we began serving and sharing them as Selma explained, the only English uttered in the entire restaurant.

"Here we have rice and meat baked inside a lotus leaf, known as *lo mai gai*," she began. It was soft and savory—a mouthful of warm comfort food. I gave Luke a sideways glance and a wink as he unwrapped his leaf and began stabbing the pork and rice with his chopsticks.

"Now this is *cha siu rao*, or bar-b-que pork buns," she said as she gracefully plucked them out of the bamboo basket and onto each of our plates.

"Already my favorite," I said as I chewed the delicate bread and savory meat filling.

"These might look scary, but they are my favorite," Selma explained as she spooned a few strangely-shaped, fried pieces onto our plates. "What is that?" Luke asked, full of anticipation and a small bit of anxiety.

"These are fried chicken feet," Selma laughed. "They are crispy and delicious!" And she crunched right into what I could only guess was one of the toes.

"Here goes nothing," I said smiling, and all three of us took a small bite of the fried foot on our plates. The dense batter gave way to a tiny metatarsal and the bone crunched in my molars. Hmmm.

"Interesting" is the word we taught Luke to use as he tried new things, and we all simultaneously responded as we finished awkwardly chewing. Thankfully, there was dessert to sweeten our mouths after the chicken feet. Moist and light butter cake squares finished off our meal, coupled with the obligatory and delicious cup of tea. While the food was not our favorite of the trip, we were especially grateful to Selma for the experience of dim sum in a local's restaurant, far from the touristy buzz of the rest of the city. We spent the afternoon walking off our meal in Hong Kong city, necks straining at skyscrapers in the financial district and squeezing into the iconic double-decker trams as daylight faded and people headed home.

I was distinctly aware that my trepidation about Asia had melted away like the afternoon sun. Hong Kong felt like the New York City of the East, and I was only sorry I had not visited sooner. As we climbed aboard a passenger ferry, the darkness was overtaken by colorfully-lit skyscrapers on both sides; bright images projected on the buildings like an adult version of Disney World. The city was alive with glowing colors reflected onto the harbor's waves, and I was thankful to be there.

On our final days in Hong Kong, we explored excellent museums and biked and hiked on the outer islands. We joined the crowds for the traditional New Year's parade one night and epic fireworks shot over the harbor the next, which we viewed from our hotel's rooftop. After a short ten days in Hong Kong, it was time to go. We were leaving the modern, clean city for something none of us had ever experienced or encountered before—the chaos and filth of India.

TRIP TIP: Several museums in Hong Kong offer free entry on Wednesdays. We visited the Science Museum and Hong Kong Museum of History in the same day since they are right next door to each other. Both are very kid-friendly.

12

India: Bending but
not Breaking

I feel obligated to caveat this chapter before it has even begun. We have learned through the years that travelers who visit India either love it or hate it. We intentionally added India to our itinerary because Mitch and I both wanted to experience it, for better or for worse. And, while we did not fall in love as many do, I have to begin by saying that the people we met while in this challenging country are among those we will count as lifelong friends—like family. These relationships were our lifeline and we are forever grateful. I used to say I would never visit India again, but as with childbirth, the harder memories fade and those that remain are precious. Seeing those friends' faces before we make it to heaven may just lead me back to India again.

We arrived in New Delhi after an eight-hour flight from Hong Kong. Armed and ready for an assault on the senses, we were surprised by the modern and clean airport. After gliding onto the first spotless metro train, we started to feel more confident, wondering when the India we had heard about was going to strike us. It was at the next stop.

We exited the airport metro train with bags in tow and emerged into the New Delhi station at exactly afternoon rush hour. Train cars were so tightly packed that we waited for two trains to come and go before we inched our way to the front of the masses. In India, there are female and male passenger cars. So I boldly separated from Mitch and

Luke and found my way to the less-crowded, but no less intimidating car for women. I was the only Westerner on board and my uncovered head and short-sleeved, V-neck t-shirt caused many to stare.

Through the dusty windows, I watched as Mitch and Luke pushed their way into the first male train car. Mitch stood out, his head and shoulders above the crowd, so we locked eyes and encouraged each other telepathically as the metro shuddered out of the station. We prepared for our two-stop journey. *Only two stops. No problem*, I told myself. But in the next few moments, I experienced the deepest fear of my life.

When the train slowed to its next stop, I watched the human wave of men spill out of the car beside me like a tsunami. Because Mitch and Luke were standing in front of the doorway, they were pulled with the tide out of the train car, separated from their bags and each other in thirty seconds of madness. I started yelling, but only the now-frightened women around me could hear my screams.

"Grab Luke! Grab Luke!" I yelled over and over, waving my arms and beating on the glass. In that moment I didn't care about our luggage, our clothes, or whether I would depart on that train without them. I just had to make sure I saw Mitch grab Luke's arm, reunited and safe.

And then, because of the mass of people waiting to board the train, just as the boys were pushed off the train they were again pushed back on. I watched through the crowd as Mitch dipped his head below their shoulders, and I breathed a heaving sigh of relief when he re-emerged with Luke in his arms. Never have I been so happy to see Luke smiling and waving at me, just feet away through the windows. I melted into a nearby seat and let the wave of nausea pass as the train jerked down the track. That experience began what would be a tumultuous three weeks in a country that pushed us to the ledge and never relented.

Stepping back from our time in India and reflecting on it months after has been a helpful exercise. Most of our friends and family asked us what was the most difficult place we visited. The answer was always the same—India. But, instead of dwelling on why we didn't like it and what made us so uncomfortable, I began to realize that this was the perfect moment to share God's amazing provision for us, not just in India at our worst, but in every other country at our best.

Our human nature often doesn't see the need to rely on God. The convenience of everything in our middle-class, American lifestyle leaves us with little need. Oftentimes we just plow through life on our own strength and will and most of it seems to work out alright. Only when life gets hard or when tragedy strikes do we recognize our need for something beyond ourselves and start to look for God. And He is always there. Right where He has been all along, walking beside us and waiting for us to give Him control over our lives.

When we reached India, we encountered a whole new level of relying on God. Getting out of our comfort zone was a purposeful exercise. We learned to rely not on ourselves in our simple, predictable lives, but to stretch our faith and trust with a grip on God's hand as He walked beside us into each country. And as we walked through the dusty streets and gawked at the filth in Delhi, we knew only He could help us see the beauty in that place.

Determined not to be intimidated or fear what is uncomfortable, we stepped off the metro the next morning and moved through the streets of Old Delhi to meet our free walking tour guide, Shruti. As the sun rose and a smoggy haze settled over the streets, we moved timidly down the sidewalk, sidestepping piles of trash as tall as Luke, and averting our eyes from stray dogs and wild monkeys picking through the rubbish for a meal.

Ramshackle two-story stucco buildings were covered in a black, smog-induced filth. Each structure was precariously perched on unsteady foundations and threatened to crumble to the ground at any moment. It reminded me of a war zone, but there had not been a battle here in half a century. Mitch tried to lighten the mood as he chuckled, "I'm not sure all the pressure washers and Clorox in the world could clean up this place."

At each corner, hundreds of electrical wires strangled one another; a jumbled knot that with one light tug would surely darken the block in an instant. Men shuffled barefoot through the streets looking for their first chai tea of the day. Women in their brightly-colored saris (the only burst of color in a brown wash-out) led their children to school by stepping around a line of beggars with hands outstretched, tattered clothes hanging from their bony frames.

The scene was post-apocalyptic, desperate, and haunting. But it seemed to be just a normal morning for these folks. How could that be? My mind wandered to my beloved Athens where my friends and family awaken each morning to a warm pot of coffee in their beautifully decorated homes, bellies full from a breakfast of their choosing, clean and well-dressed in an outfit of hundreds from their walk-in closets. That was our everyday routine. I was stunned at how vastly different the morning I was witnessing was from my own.

Of course I kept all of these thoughts to myself as we met Shruti, the young owner of the walking tour company, and began walking around the Old Town. I admired her wide smile, energetic pride, and knowledge of the city's history; once a vibrant marketplace and community, now a crumbling remnant of itself. She guided us through streets and alleyways, giving us a good history and commentary on the state of the city. The trash piles weren't normally that high, she explained matter-of-factly. There had been a two-week sanitation strike. Somehow that didn't settle my concerns.

We saw religious buildings, five different belief systems on the same road, all providing food and shelter to the overwhelming number of needy. In a back alley that I would only bravely enter with my six-foot-six-inch husband, Shruti introduced us to a gentle, old man selling chai tea from a portable tea kettle resting on a cinderblock table. We sipped the warm, sweet drink and listened to stories of generations of families. Families who once lived in these close quarters, but have now moved beyond the Old Town and into the sprawl of modern Delhi.

After the tour, we, as usual, invited Shruti to join us for lunch.

She suggested a cafeteria a few miles away and generously negotiated with two *tuk-tuk* drivers to get us there. Mitch and Luke climbed aboard and I rode behind them with Shruti. The bicycle-driven *tuk-tuks* were primitive compared to our zippy, gasoline-powered rides in Thailand, but with all the smog and traffic already choking the streets, I was thankful for the slower, emission-free excursion.

We had endured walking for two hours in a city I hoped I would never have to return to. And just as my fake smile began to crack in front of our dear tour guide, Luke turned around with a genuine grin, ear to ear, to yell back to me, "Mom, isn't this fun? We just saw a cow in the street and almost ran into a taxi!" His sweet innocence and willingness to take in as positive what I saw as negative was the refreshing boost I needed to make it through lunch and back on the metro. Once in our hotel room, we collapsed from sensory overload, exhaustion, and disbelief.

I wish I could say the rest of our time in Delhi was better, but two days later we were ready to escape the city of seventeen million and head to the "smaller" city of Jaipur. Home to only 2.5 million people, Jaipur sits in the highly-touted Rajasthan region and boasts colorful castles, forts, and tigers. The scene that awaited us was still difficult, but it was here we met strangers who became friends—fellow Christians who greeted us like family.

While I had found Elephant Nature Park on the internet, our opportunity to volunteer in India came through the church where I grew up in Marietta, Georgia. A Baptist mega-church focused on global missions, there were opportunities around the world for us to connect with mission partners. I think God knew we would be struggling in India, so he put the Luke family in our path. Even their unusual, non-traditional surname was a wink from God that He was looking out for us.

"You will join us for Bible Study tonight," Sanjeev Luke stated without question as we stood drinking coffee in the ninety-degree heat after church. It was the morning after our arrival. We had had a long (and late) night on the train from Delhi. But we were energized by the idea of meeting new friends at the mission church in the Bani Park neighborhood of Jaipur. Christians make up only 4 percent of the population in India, and while they are not necessarily persecuted, they are somewhat shunned from the rest of society.

"We will pick you up at seven o'clock," he continued. "No need to eat dinner before. We will eat together at our friends' house."

We had a first date with our Indian friends. Little did we know that when they picked us up later that evening, it would be in a tiny Tata Nano—a sedan smaller than a Ford Focus hatchback. Their family of four unloaded with welcoming hugs outside our hotel. As we began to climb in, I wondered where all of us would sit. Like a clown car at the circus, Mitch folded into the front seat beside Sanjeev (both men more than six feet tall with their knees to their noses). Sanjeev, a music teacher, was bringing along his guitar to play for the group; so (un)naturally that fit right between Mitch's cramped legs.

Archana and her two children, Anushka and Akkoo, opened the back doors and slid inside. Akkoo, nine years old and nearly as tall as his mother, climbed onto her lap and Anushka gingerly squeezed into the middle of the backseat. That left about twelve inches for Luke and me. We followed their lead and Luke sat on my lap, no seatbelts to be seen. The silent praying began as Sanjeev peeled away and merged onto the eight-lane highway.

We happened to be visiting during Lent and these church families met in small groups every weeknight for the entire forty days to read and study the Bible, eat dinner, and spend time together. It was a wonderful glimpse into an Indian home and when we arrived we inhaled the authentic, cultural experience as strongly as the simmering curry on the stove.

The faithful Luke family picked us up every night that week, and we became closer to the group as we rotated to everyone's home, ate meals with them, and read the Bible. As it happens, the singing and teaching were all done in Hindi, as was the church service the previous Sunday. So Mitch, Luke, and I sat respectfully and did our best to read along in English while enjoying the ambience of new friends.

Another church member, Sam, asked us to accompany him during the weekdays to several private schools where he administered English classes. Middle- and upper-class families paid a large portion of their meager salaries to ensure their children would receive a good education and compete in the global economy. Mitch and I were asked to speak to the students about the importance of learning English, explaining how it expands opportunities for jobs beyond their homeland.

We were both quite nervous and tried to prepare a meaningful message, but we were not sure our words would translate literally and figuratively with the young students. I hoped they would even understand our American accents.

At the first school we were met by the headmaster, a strong and confident woman. She greeted us warmly and enthusiastically thanked us for our time. She led us through the building toward the play yard outdoors; this is where assemblies were held each morning. Standing before us were nearly 300 students, some as young as four years old, dressed in identical red uniforms and standing in rows as stiffly and perfectly as if they were practicing a military drill. We followed the headmaster to the makeshift stage and sat behind her as she approached the podium.

"Good morning, children!" she bellowed.

"Good morning, teacher!" they loudly responded.

"This morning after our pledge, you will hear from two guests who have come all the way from America to speak to you. I know you will give them your undivided attention and respect."

A few upperclassmen joined the faculty onstage and led their classmates through what I believe was their country's pledge of allegiance in Hindi. The students made a few announcements in English about upcoming activities on campus and then they glanced at us as if it was our turn. As I gazed out among the crowd, I realized they were going to stand at attention throughout this entire assembly. Not one had fallen out of line, started to wiggle, or even shifted from side to side. I was blown away! My child couldn't stand still for thirty seconds, much less the thirty minutes these babies were about to endure. I made a mental note to ask the headmaster later what her trick was and I secretly prayed there was no corporal punishment involved.

Mitch and I briefly addressed the young crowd. We talked about our education and how important it was to study hard, do your best, and always strive to achieve one's goals. We talked about our travels and how we had ended up in Jaipur, India, in their schoolyard. I'm not really sure we provided any great service to them, but I guess the intention to inspire was achieved or at least the novelty of an American family was enough to keep their interest. Our friend Sam seemed happy with our messages and after the children were dismissed to their classrooms, we toured the school and visited two others over the coming days. I wondered if this was how politicians felt on their campaign stops, giving the same speeches and hoping to connect with strangers, smiling, and shaking hands until their cheeks began to ache. It was an unusual way to volunteer, but when we offered ourselves that was what they requested. We served them as best we could and fine tuned our public speaking skills in Rajasthan.

After a week of visiting schools during the day and clown car cruising at night, we thought it might be fun to take a weekend excursion outside of the city; trading the smog and noise for wildlife. We booked a tiger safari at Ranthambore National Park a few hours away and hoped to uncover the beauty Rajasthan is known for in a more remote and exotic part of the region.

As we drove out of the bustling city and into the desert, I felt the pressure slowly lift. It was difficult to escape the intensity of India, no matter where you went. Since our arrival, I had found myself becoming increasingly introverted; retreating into myself to escape the loud, confusing, and oftentimes dismal views around us. I even reached a point when I didn't want to leave the hotel because it was mentally exhausting to face the outside world.

As we continued driving toward Ranthambore, we encountered camels, wild dogs, and pigs sauntering along the road. Watching the sun rise, I was able to breathe deeper and relax as we pointed toward the dusty hills of Sawai Madhopur where our safari weekend would begin. Upon arriving at our "four-star" hotel, we were greeted by a pack of pigs nosing their way through a pile of trash, a veritable welcoming committee outside the wrought iron gates that indicated we were not completely escaping the rough fabric of India like we'd hoped. That's when I understood there was no escaping it. Maybe there are other parts of the country that feel, smell, and sound differently. But a realization washed over me that I needed to accept and embrace what surrounded me, because otherwise it would just suck me under.

My change in attitude was timely. We were picked up an hour later by our safari guide in an open 4x4 Jeep. The Jeep rattled through town, then to the outskirts, and finally we entered Ranthambore National Park, home to the elusive Indian tiger.

"To see a tiger is very special," the guide began. "There are only fifty-five tigers in all 150 square miles of our park and we will search mightily for them. But never fear, if we don't see one we will surely see many animals including deer, monkeys, antelope, and peacocks."

The landscape was rugged, mountainous, and dry. I was surprised how much Northern India reminded me of the Middle East with its unrelenting dust, arid climate, and lack of green. We jolted along in the backseat of the Jeep, Luke once again grinning from ear to ear. The more extreme the vehicle, the better the ride, in his mind.

After a few hours through the winding paths up and down the rocky hills of the park, we approached a steep ravine and slowed to a stop. Our guide climbed out with his binoculars in hand and peered into the crevasse below. Two hundred yards away a mama tiger was lounging lazily on the rocks, basking in the sun while her two cubs played nearby. What a sight! The enormous cat was far enough from us that our quiet squeals of joy didn't disturb or alarm her.

We observed the scene for several minutes, snapping hundreds of photos, before our guide picked up his radio and sent word to his colleagues in other vehicles that he had made the sighting. As we slowly drove on, several Jeeps full of anxious tourists sped onto our path and overtook the spot for their own viewing delight. We were the envy of the other hotel guests later that evening when Luke shared the excitement of spotting a family of jungle cats.

Our weekend away was a nice change of pace and we returned to Jaipur with renewed spirits and a willingness to spend our final days making the most of what we encountered. We switched hotels to one that had a rooftop restaurant—a sanctuary above the madness offering a wide range of food and consistent internet connectivity. We became regulars at the Peacock Rooftop of the Hotel Pearl Palace; enjoying the cooler mornings over a lazy breakfast and later watching the sun set across tile rooftops with glasses of wine in hand. We also traded *tuk-tuks* for Uber, willingly paying the extra dollar or two for air-conditioning and closed windows.

On our last night in Jaipur, the Luke family invited us over for a home-cooked meal. Mitch towered over Archana in her kitchen as she stirred and spiced the *daal*. He rolled out the *chappati* bread, learning how to cook it masterfully on the open fire so it would toast but not burn. We did not sit down to eat until 10:00 p.m.— apparently a normal hour for their family and the culture. Archana served us a beautiful meal and we enjoyed our time with them, flipping through their wedding album over coffee, and learning the age-old Indian wedding traditions. Archana and Sanjeev were so genuinely hospitable and kind, it was overwhelming.

Being inside the Luke's home was an intimate experience. I was once again reminded of how materially blessed we are back home. Their house was large by Indian standards, with three bedrooms, a living room, and kitchen. It was spacious and comfortable but had sparse furnishings and no decor hanging on the cement walls.

Their dog barked incessantly the entire visit and after a while I asked, "Archana, where is your dog? Does he want to come in?"

"Oh no, dear. He's on the roof. He lives up there, but he'd rather be down here meeting our guests. Don't mind him."

I'm not sure if the neighbors were used to the dog's noise, or if he was drowned out by the traffic on the road nearby, but he continued to howl the entire night and was never seen.

As it neared midnight, I was over-stimulated, tired, and ready to say our goodbyes. Archana came into the room with gifts for all of us, including a hand-made navy blue *kurta* tunic with beautiful gold stitching for me. I was overwhelmed with gratitude and started to cry. These lovely people who live in such a harsh place showed an abundance of love and acceptance to us, who were virtual strangers. Our friendship, while birthed in a city I hoped never to see again, was binding and transcended this earthly place. There is no doubt the Luke family will remain in our lives forever.

Our final days in India were spent on a pilgrimage to the Taj Mahal, one of the seven wonders of the modern world. A majestic and impressive white marble mausoleum, it was erected for emperor Shah Jahan's wife to be laid to rest alongside the Yamuna river. We visited the site at sunrise and watched the sun bathe it in soft pink light before masses of tourists arrived.

After three long weeks, India had totaled us. Luke began coughing from what I could only deduce was irritation from the constant inhalation of dirt and grime. We began sleeping longer hours and taking naps during the day—our bodies literally exhausted from the endurance of it all. We became veritable hermits in our hotel in Agra during the final days of our stay in the country. We finished the "Northern Triangle" while on a train back to Delhi. There we caught a long flight southwest to Africa and our next stop—Nairobi, Kenya.

TRIP TIP: Cooking classes introduced the local cuisine and provided an opportunity for us to learn how to make a few dishes. Our cooking class in Jaipur was led by a former hotel chef in his personal home. It was a wonderful experience, a five-course meal, and a very reasonable price.

Snorkeling in the Great Barrier Reef, Australia

Scooping poo at Elephant Nature Park, Thailand

Perfecting fresh spring rolls at one of the
many cooking classes in Southeast Asia

Sunrise at Angkor Wat temple, Cambodia

Another sunrise visit to one of the wonders
of the world—the Taj Mahal in India

Teaching Uno to the kids at First Love, Kenya

Second grade in Nairobi, one of the
many schools Luke visited

A camel ride among the Pyramids of Giza in Egypt

Riding bicycles—one of our favorite traveling
past times—outside Istanbul, Turkey

The spectacular view from our hot air
balloon ride in Cappadocia, Turkey

13

Kenya: Finding Joy

Welcome to Kenya. Bright blue skies. Crisp green trees. Piercing spring sun. The dull sky we had left behind in India was stripped clean, bathed in blinding light, and a symbol of restorative hope for all three of us. The taxi ride from the airport to Nairobi's suburban town of Karen took us alongside the world's only urban national safari park. I looked out over a beautiful savannah and there in the distance was a lone giraffe. Even though we had endured a twelve-hour flight, I already felt refreshed and thankful to be in the heart of Africa.

First Love orphanage—a home for adopted children from the slums of nearby Kibera—was our destination, another anchor of our trip. My mother had visited First Love many times throughout the last ten years to serve more than 100 children who lived there, and she and my father financially sponsor one of the boys, Richard.

Since Richard is close in age to Luke, my mom always asks Luke for his help in picking out clothes, shoes, and toys to take to Richard each year. We naturally felt that Richard was part of our family and we couldn't wait to meet him, his brothers, and sisters in person.

"*Jambo*, my friends! *Jambo!*"

Director Chris Okuna greeted us at the orphanage gates. He had a wide smile and a youthful but patriarchal demeanor.

"We are so glad you have arrived! The children are just coming home from school so you can greet them."

We exited the taxi and looked around, taking in the manicured lawn and lush landscape. Bright pink flowers, yellow and green variegated bushes, budding trees—this was a glimpse of heaven, a place of refuge for children who had come from the pits of hell. Many were orphans, but some had parents or grandparents who simply could no longer care for them. First Love offered a safe home, food, clean water, and education for kids lost in the dire circumstances of poverty and neglect. The sun shone brightly on this place of hope, life, and love, and our own battered souls were eager to be refreshed as we met the joyful faces walking through the gates from school.

Service to others is oftentimes more rewarding for you than it is for those you serve. After weeks of slogging through a country that never seemed to fit us, we were immediately wrapped in a warm blanket of comfort and affection as we introduced ourselves to the children and employees of First Love. We were there to volunteer our time and talents, but Chris' main objective for us was simple.

"Just spend time with them," he said warmly. "They want to play with you, talk to you, and give and receive hugs. It's pretty simple."

A simple life was what we had been striving for along this entire journey, and it was epitomized in our ten days at the orphanage. Our mornings were quiet and slow while the children were at school. We caught up on correspondence and schoolwork and watched anxiously out the window of our second-story apartment housed in the girl's dormitory for the first pre-schoolers to arrive home after lunch. We ran excitedly to meet them as they kicked off their leather shoes and changed into play clothes.

On the playground with soft grass under bare feet, I turned the jump rope thousands of rotations as each young child ran in and out, chanting as we counted. To my amazement, Kofi— a spirited young boy—jumped 850 times during his turn! Joyce beamed, showing off her wide smile as she clambered across the monkey bars. Anne, petite and shy, batted her eyelashes like a delicate butterfly as she quietly asked for another push on the swing. Slevia showed spunk as she learned how to deftly throw a frisbee, never before having seen the plastic toy. Young Emily loved to hold my hand and led me to the covered table where she braided my hair proudly. Day after day, each child's beautiful and unique personality was revealed as we played.

When the older kids came home from school later in the afternoon, we observed them diligently wash their clothes in large tubs of well water then lay them flat in the grass to dry in the sun. The boys shined their shoes as they had become dusty on the walk home. Every single day they shined their shoes. Mitch joined the boys who played soccer in the field behind the dormitories, strategically avoiding the cow patties that were left behind by the four milking cows allowed to graze there. The property was abuzz with happy sounds of playing, laughter and freedom—the way a child's life should be. My heart exploded with happiness for these kids and their second chance at an abundant life. How encouraging to see such innocence and joy after enduring years of hardship and cruelty.

The First Love children had found hope in their new circumstances thanks to the love and support of Chris and his wife, Irene, who began their mission by bringing food and support to children inside Nairobi's Kibera slums; children who were barely existing in desolate conditions. After many years, they created First Love as the children's way out of destitution. The government works with Chris and Irene and relies on them to take kids in dire need of shelter and a stable environment. For Chris and Irene, it is a life's work and a personal calling, supported by an American nonprofit that has similar homes around the world.

As we spent time with the children day in and day out, I was overcome with wonder as to how they were so well adjusted and joyful despite what they had gone through. The way of life at First Love is built upon the love and teachings of the Christian faith.

Through singing, Bible study, and prayer, the kids are given an opportunity to live and grow as followers of Jesus.

Each evening at six o'clock, we witnessed the full display of joy and gratitude for the second chance they had been given at life. Without any prompting from adults or caregivers, all of the children gathered in the dining hall. To the fast beat of the traditional African drum, singing filled the space. Dancing, clapping, and shouts of joyful noise echoed through the property as they chanted upbeat tunes of praise. After several songs, an older teen read from the Bible and talked to his peers about what the verses meant. It could be a story or a pointed lesson and there were always questions asked to the group, ensuring listening ears were tuned in to the message.

To my surprise, multiple hands shot up every night. The children were eager to engage in conversation and deepen their understanding of what was being taught. These children exuded a spirit of profound thankfulness for all they had been given and not even one seemed to take it for granted. Their dedication to their chores, devotional time with God, and focus on their studies expressed gratitude far beyond anything they could verbally convey.

Our experience at First Love was a great opportunity to teach Luke that many children around the world do not have the same material luxuries and conveniences we have. We accompanied the kids to school one morning and sat in the second-grade classroom made of cinderblocks, broken windows, and old wooden desks. The playground was a dirt yard with no equipment. The facilities were dire. But the children were learning many of the same subjects Luke was, and the lessons looked and sounded very familiar. The games they played outside during their break were universal and Luke joined in, happy to run off some pent up energy from a morning inside. He did not seem the least bit fazed that his surroundings were not like school back home. They were happy. And he was happy.

I was thankful these differences weren't affecting him and he was seeing through to the people themselves, instead of their circumstances. We want Luke to grow up without many of the prejudices and stereotypes that keep us from connecting with people from all walks of life.

Nighttime was dedicated to the kids' studies and they diligently focused on homework from dinner until lights-out at 10:00 p.m. Mitch helped the older kids with their math and science and Luke and I waited for the younger children to finish so we could play Uno with them. It was the first time they had heard of the card game and they quickly caught on. We would often have fifteen to twenty kids circled around the table sharing hands dealt to them and eagerly playing their cards. Luke became overwhelmed many nights, not understanding the chaos and excitement of what is normally a fairly tame and quiet game. He struggled being around so many children, which is understandable as an only child. But I pushed him to stay with me every night instead of allowing him to retreat into our room, knowing that every moment he spent out of his comfort zone might grow his patience and selflessness.

One night he came to me nearly in tears, "Mom, please let me go upstairs. These kids are bothering me and I've had enough."

"I know it's hard, Luke," I gently replied. "But they are so happy to have you here. They are just excited and don't know how to express it."

"They keep playing the game wrong and they won't listen to me when I try to explain it," he continued. His voice raised an octave and I could see his lower lip quivering.

"Listen, sometimes it's not our place to make everything perfect," I said. "We are just here to be friends and show them love. It's hard after a long day, but I want you to try just a few minutes longer."

I didn't want to spell out exactly how difficult their lives were. I hoped he could sense it and understand that our discomfort was just a sliver of the pain they had suffered. Selflessly loving the unfamiliar and stretching ourselves to care for people we don't know builds the character I want my son to embody. Maybe this night would be the first of many life experiences in putting the needs of others before himself.

Our final days at First Love were bittersweet since we had built relationships and grown to love the kids. On our last night we decided to host a party and got a ride with Chris down to Nakumatt—the Kenyan version of Walmart—for several large tubs of vanilla and chocolate ice cream. After supper, Chris announced to the kids that we had a special treat for them. Sweets of any kind after dinner were rare, so when we started scooping the cold and creamy dessert, eyes widened and a few squeals of delight were heard around the dining hall. As I passed out the bowls and spoons, the little ones looked at each other in dismay.

"Do you not like ice cream?" I asked worriedly. I had not even considered that it might give them a tummy ache or worse, an allergic reaction.

"We've never had ice cream, Miss Suzanne," one of the sweet girls replied. "What does it taste like?"

"Oh, it's delicious!" I exclaimed, with tears in my eyes. "You'll like it, I'm sure!"

How could one of our ubiquitous American treats be completely unknown to children across the world? It was another small reminder of how far from home we were and how different the lives of those surrounding us had been. I vowed that night to return again and again to First Love and never take for granted even the smallest blessings we had been given.

While we were in Africa we thought it a must to visit a national park and witness the majesty of the animals on safari. We researched many options and decided to give the "tented camp" a try since it fit our budget and sounded a bit adventurous. I'm not one who loves to sleep on the ground outside. I wish I were, because a night under the stars sounds magical, but when I wake up with an achy back and foggy-headed from lack of sleep, I don't enjoy the activities the next day brings. Mitch had to do a bit of convincing that the tented safari camp was up to my sleeping standards, and so we booked three nights at the Ilkeliani Camp in the Maasai Mara Game Reserve. It far exceeded our expectations. We realized our "budget" decision was actually one of the grander accommodations of the entire trip.

Our driver, Joseph, arrived at First Love early the next morning and Luke just about had a fit when he saw that the SUV was a Land Cruiser. Luke hopped right in and began asking Joseph for stats and details about the vehicle. Perfectly poised with his head out the open window, Luke eagerly watched the city melt away as we drove five hours northwest into the remote grasslands of the Maasai Mara savannah. The Ilkeliani Camp was nestled alongside a river on the outskirts of the game preserve. As our hosts greeted us, they walked us down a path to reveal a spacious tent built upon gorgeous hardwood floors. The two-bed tent was connected to a lovely tiled bathroom with a proper shower, sink, and toilet. *This is my kind of camping!* I thought.

After we had washed up from the long and dusty drive, Joseph met us once again to take us out for our first evening game drive. We were met by giraffes, warthogs, zebras, and gazelles from the very moment we drove into the reserve and marveled as the sun set beyond the hills while the animals roamed freely. We spent the next days searching for more elusive animals like lions, cheetahs, leopards, and elephants. Joseph's scouting skills were honed from a lifetime career as a safari guide and he thrilled us every time we rounded a corner and revealed a family of romping lion cubs or a herd of hippos bathing in the river.

Because we were there in March, many babies had just been born. One morning, we saw a gazelle Joseph estimated to be only about thirty minutes old. It could barely walk, wobbling and leaning into its mother. We spent an afternoon watching from afar as two lionesses led their six cubs across a field then laid in the sun while the babies climbed all over each other and frolicked around the base of a tree. One evening, after a long day of searching, Mitch spotted an elusive leopard in the crook of a tree at least 250 yards away. It was a spectacular find. After several excited calls on the radio, many other guides rushed from miles away to catch a glimpse.

There is nothing in the world like riding across the savannah with the wind whipping your face, exotic animals alongside you at every turn. Photographs and *National Geographic* documentaries try to do it justice, but taking a safari is something too visceral not to be experienced personally. It is magical, and our full hearts were now overflowing with love for the country. Kenya had found its way into my soul—once experienced, never forgotten.

TRIP TIP: If you are traveling to volunteer with children in another country, ask your host about appropriate gifts, toys, or games to bring. Oftentimes there are simple favorites that need replacing or you can introduce new games for kids of all ages that are easy to pack like Uno or frisbee.

14

Egypt: Keeping it Loose

Mitch had been monitoring the latest news and political climate as we headed toward the Middle East. We were also receiving updates through our U.S. State Department STEP app on the unrest and war in Syria. Our planned itinerary was to fly north from Kenya to Turkey. Once again, we realized that the path would take us directly over another wonder of the world we wanted to explore—the Egyptian pyramids.

Since the Arab Spring of 2012, Egypt had been through severe political and military unrest. I still reflect on our decision to go to Egypt and wonder if it was a smart, safe decision. Because of the instability in the country's capital, travelers and tourists had virtually stopped visiting Cairo and the pyramids of Giza. But since there had not been major demonstrations, bombings, or widespread unrest for many months, after a lot of prayer and discernment, we decided to make a three-night pit stop to explore Egypt's ancient history.

There was a moment on the flight from Nairobi to Cairo when I was overcome with emotion. *I am on a plane from Kenya to Egypt. On a trip around the world!* I pinched my skin and marveled over the spark of an idea that was coming to fruition before my very eyes. Luke told me he punched himself in the arm sometimes to make sure he wasn't dreaming. We did dream it, but it became a reality. I vowed on that flight to continue appreciating every moment—big and small, fun and tedious, awe-inspiring and annoying. We were given a gift, an answered prayer, the desire of our hearts. And it was stunning.

Driving from the airport to our hotel in Giza, I had hoped to feel the exotic vibes of Indiana Jones and the romantic explorers of the nineteenth century, but what we saw were dusty traffic jams and miles of high-rise apartment blocks baking in the North African sun. I was thankful we had chosen to stay in Giza, nearly fifteen miles from downtown Cairo. It made sense for us to be near the pyramids, and they were literally outside our window when we arrived to our hotel room.

We booked a two-day private tour for our excursions to Giza, Memphis, and Saqqara to ensure we did not get sidetracked in the wrong part of town. It turned out to be a wonderful investment for our peace of mind and educational experience.

The next morning, we met our guide, Ashraf. Ashraf quickly impressed us with his knowledge of ancient Egypt and the sites we were meant to see in the coming days. A tour guide for twenty-five years, he was wise and spoke excellent English. With several children and grandchildren of his own, he showed great patience with Luke as he asked more than 52,000 questions about everything we encountered under the hot Egyptian sun.

Our first stop was the Giza pyramid complex, just a stone's throw from our hotel. We got an early start, but it wouldn't be necessary as we would learn throughout our visit. The tourism industry had suffered greatly due to the country's recent turmoil and we were literally the only visitors for much of the morning. But for us it was an added benefit—I loved being the only family walking quietly through the sacred grounds without the disturbance of other tourists.

We gazed up at the towering Great Pyramid, shielding our eyes from the bright morning light. Walking around the base, you began to get a sense of the magnitude of the structure and the extraordinary feat of building such a monument. Luke stood at the base of the massive carved stones, each almost as tall as he was. Above him soared multitudes of rows made up of thousand-pound boulders, chiseled masterfully and placed expertly as had never been done before. Even in its decay, it was a breathtaking masterpiece.

Nearby, we visited the famous Sphinx, a smaller watchman than we expected. We walked among the lesser-known tombs in the area that don't always make the history books but are full of captivating archaeological tales. After a while, Ashraf drove us further from the pyramids for an opportunity to ride camels through the desert with a view of the three structures. I can't believe we were almost too cheap to part with $25 USD for the ride that included a photo opportunity. We were being conscious of the added expense of having a private tour and were trying to stick to our budget. Thankfully, we thought better of it and embraced the moment. Our happy camels, one of whom Luke named Mike from the silly "Hump Day" Geico commercials, lumbered us out to a vista point and the twenty-minute excursion produced some of my favorite photos of the entire trip.

From Giza we drove to Memphis, and my memory of Egyptian history began to fail. Ashraf was an invaluable source for details and context that would have been missed by us if we had been traveling there alone. Once the capital, Memphis is now just an open-air museum with artifacts and remnants on display. Several statues of Ramses II are still in good condition and we tried to digest the magnitude and complexities of Egypt's history of rulers and kings.

After an outdoor lunch in a café meant for hundreds but catering only to us (another reminder of tourism's sad state of affairs), we headed to Saqqara, our third and final stop of the afternoon. Because Saqqara is further out in the desert and away from any modern civilization, it felt very authentic and easier to imagine the pyramids in their original glory. My favorite part of this stop was going inside several of the tombs and viewing hieroglyphics up close. The tombs of lesser ministers were open and we walked through chamber after chamber, admiring the artwork and ancient text carved and painted on the stone walls.

With brains full of historical information and eyes soaked with ancient imagery, our sunburned and worn-out souls found refreshment back in the hotel pool. Due to the long day of touring, we didn't venture far from the hotel, opting for a traditional kebab supper nearby. We woke early the next morning ready for another full day of sightseeing.

On our second tour day with Ashraf, we braved Cairo's traffic and crowds for a visit to the world-renowned Museum of Egyptian Antiquities. It was bursting with thousands of relics from the Old, Middle, and New Kingdom pyramids. We witnessed artifacts and sarcophagi found in the tombs we had visited just the day before in Giza and Saqqara, giving context to these riches that had been stowed away with the dead thousands of years ago. An entire floor was dedicated to King Tutankhamun's material wealth. Luke was fascinated as he explored the small child's toys, beds, and clothes packed away for him to use in the afterlife.

After our morning visit to the museum we saw a few other highlights of Cairo, including the military fortress, royal family home, and mosque. The mosque was built in the same style as the Blue Mosque in Istanbul and we would later compare the two.

We strolled through the Coptic ("Egyptian") Christian neighborhood and visited the church that sheltered Joseph, Mary, and Jesus when they escaped Herod's terror just after Jesus' birth; another fascinating piece of history I had only read about in books and never imagined I would witness for myself.

Ashraf capped off our second day with a trip to the famous bazaar, a treasure trove of cheap souvenirs that Luke adored and I tolerated. He opted for an overpriced metal pyramid and enjoyed bargaining the price down with the local merchant. Afterwards as we sipped tea at an outdoor café, Mitch and I agreed it was the right decision to make a short stop in this crumbling, yet famous, ancient city.

One of the best lessons I learned in Egypt was *sometimes you just don't know.* I was never sure about whether we should stop in Cairo. My gut wasn't telling me anything concretely and neither research nor news monitoring swayed me one way or the other. For many people, just the fact that they have to monitor the situation means they would rather not go. Totally understandable. For us, it was knowing we may never get back to that part of the world again as a family that swayed us. We wanted to take advantage of seeing every historical landmark we could possibly squeeze in. And although we tried to make smart, educated choices about our itinerary, we could only ask and trust God to keep us safe. Sometimes you just don't know if you are making the right decision, but I did know confidently that we were being protected by prayer. That thread of uncertainty combined with prayerful trust carried us into Turkey where we would encounter our closest brush with real danger to date.

TRIP TIP: Viator is a great website and third-party booking resource when you want a guided tour or excursion. Owned by TripAdvisor, we found the prices to be reasonable, the user reviews helpful, and the outfits they connected us with very reputable. They offer thousands of unique excursions in nearly 2,500 destinations around the world.

15

Turkey:
First World Problems

Without intending to, it seems we had given up the first world for Lent. After more than forty days in India, Kenya, and Egypt, we were anxiously anticipating a clean, modern, and beautiful European city when we arrived in Istanbul. And it delivered. We loved the walkable cobblestone streets and sidewalk cafes, the beautiful parks and historic sites, the kind and friendly people. Istanbul was vibrant—full of delicious tastes, fresh air, and wild color.

But with the first world came the problems it faces. Because of its proximity to Syria and recent government unrest, it too had been a volatile country that we debated skipping. There were terrorist threats and incidents happening on the eastern side of the country near the Syrian border and in the capital of Ankara. But with fourteen million people residing in Istanbul, we got a sense that the odds were in our favor if we acted street smart and avoided crowded areas, public transportation, and steered clear of any protests. However, there was a heightened sense of awareness and unease when we emerged from our Airbnb apartment in the Sultanahmet neighborhood the first morning.

We had been greeted early with a knock at the door by our friendly host, Hikmet. The one-bedroom apartment was in a great location and with a full kitchen and pullout couch for Luke, we were excited to settle in for the week.

"May I serve you breakfast on the rooftop?" Hikmet offered proudly, seeming to enjoy his hosting duties and going above and beyond, in my opinion. In our experience, Airbnb hosts ran the gamut from totally absent and leaving a key with instructions to serving as local tour guide and providing a stocked refrigerator upon arrival. However, a catered breakfast on the terrace overlooking the Bosphorus was a first!

"Welcome to our beautiful city, the gateway from Europe to Asia," Hikmet offered as he cooked our eggs over a camping stove in the makeshift kitchen beside our sunny table. "We are so happy to have visitors. Many people are concerned about coming here so tourism is down and my business has been slow."

We learned Hikmet was not only an Airbnb owner, but ran a local travel agency nearby.

"I hope you will allow me to escort you to the Hippodrome after breakfast so you can see our iconic Blue Mosque and the Hagia Sophia in the morning light."

We could not pass up Hikmet's generous hospitality. It's always nice to get some assistance from a local when navigating a city on the first morning, so after a simple but delightful meal of eggs, feta cheese, and toast with honey, we descended into the streets and followed Hikmet a few blocks toward the soaring domes and spires of the historic religious sites.

The police presence was immediately apparent as uniformed and plain-clothed officers loitered in small groups around the fountains and pedestrian-only boulevards that outlined the area for visitors. We said goodbye to Hikmet, wondering whether it was safe to stroll the area. The bright blue sky invited us to explore and I was drawn in by the tulip-lined gardens and clean walkways with benches to sit and enjoy the views. Although I had nothing to compare to, I felt like the area was unusually uncrowded. A few families and other tourists were around, but it was quiet and calm.

"I think we should visit the Basilica Cistern," Mitch announced. It was one of the lesser-known sites but one that intrigued us. "I'd like to get a better feel for the security at tourist attractions before we enter the more-famous Hagia Sofia or Blue Mosque."

It was a logical train of thought, but I was immediately struck by how weird it was to try and make decisions based on a threat we didn't know enough about, or whether there was a real threat at all. We would come to learn later that spring as we made our way through the larger cities of Europe that it was hard to balance the uncertainty of safety with the resolve not to alter plans or live in fear of a terrorist threat.

Many of the cities we would visit had a police presence I had never experienced on previous trips abroad, but this was the current reality of our world and Western Europe was on high alert. As a parent, I was more sensitive to the potential threats and dangers because of my concern and obligation to keep Luke safe. There seemed to be no right answer to finding the balance of awareness and fear. We tried to navigate it as best we could and enjoy Istanbul and all its beauty, but I had a constant feeling of unease.

The Basilica Cistern, although not the icon of its neighboring must-see sites of the city, became my favorite. It was the first time I had experienced such a marvel of ancient underground architecture. The masterful Roman engineering descends under the modern streets of Istanbul into a dark and cavernous vessel that was once used to hold 80,000 cubic meters of water for the city's residents. Istanbul (then Constantinople) was the capital of the Roman/ Byzantine Empire, named after Constantine the Great. During the reign of Emperor Justinian in the sixth century, he built the city to be a rival of the former capital in Rome. We had already walked through the ruins of the Hippodrome, a chariot-racing course that was the sporting and social center of the city in Justinian's heyday. But the Basilica Cistern had been restored to its former glory so as not to be left to the imagination. Three hundred thirty-eight massive Roman columns held up the ceiling and we walked above the remaining shallow water on decking to see the expanse of the space. Light from dim spotlights reflected on the water, multiplying the appearance of the columns into a beautiful, artistic display. We were among several visitors who were all hushed throughout our visit, walking reverently through the columns trying to wrap our brains around the strength, beauty, and sheer difficulty of creating such a structure 1,500 years ago. It was quite captivating.

Back in the bright daylight, we grabbed the first of many delicious meals in a nearby Turkish restaurant. Known for their meat kebabs, fresh grilled vegetables, and tangy salads, I savored every dish and vowed to cook as little as possible in our apartment since the choices on the streets were delightful and the merchants so welcoming.

After lunch, we were more emboldened to visit Hagia Sofia, a beautiful church turned mosque turned museum. We realized, as experienced at the Basilica Cistern, that the security presence was intensely heightened at the most popular sites. There were metal detectors, body wands, and multiple officers giving us a sense of reassurance with smiles and deliberate calm. We felt safer inside the tourist attractions than anywhere else in the city.

Hagia Sofia houses a voluminous domed ceiling and an interesting conglomeration of religious iconography from Christians and Muslims. Delicate mosaics of Christ are on display alongside graphic lettering from the Koran. We walked through the museum quietly appreciating the stunning works of art and architecture, awe-inspired again by the origins from as far back as 537 A.D. Since stopping in Egypt, world history was beginning to come to life with an intensity that I had never before experienced. This corner of the world took me back farther than any church or ruin in Western Europe. You could feel the layer upon layer of ancient civilization that are still part of the fabric of their culture today.

Feeling more confident to explore, the next day we spent an adventurous afternoon in the Grand Bazaar, the mother ship to all shopaholics. Its maze of booths and the historic spice market nearby were alive with the smells and colorful sights one would expect from the centuries-old place of trade. Luke spotted a beautiful wooden chess set and expertly bargained the friendly young merchant down to a reasonable price. It was a unique travel set that collapsed in half with a case underneath to hold its magnetic pieces. Mitch insisted we also buy a selection of spices, their fragrance too tempting to walk past.

We stopped at a small café for lunch and the line of cooks behind the counter greeted us boisterously as I attempted to order, butchering the Turkish language and laughing at myself. The men eased my embarrassment by offering a few samples and we bonded over the universal language of food. I'm not sure we could ever find the tiny restaurant again in the myriad of entrances and exits to the Bazaar, but if you find yourself outside gate eighteen, be sure to make time for a stop at Donerci Sahin Usta.

It wasn't just the food that drew us into Istanbul, but its people. The local residents exuded a warmth to visitors, radiating pride for their cosmopolitan city that also held a storied history. The dichotomies of ancient city and modern metropolis reminded us of Paris and London, and each person we met seemed intent on showing off their corner of the world. We engaged with several locals throughout the week and later reflected on their kindness.

One morning we explored the Topkapi Palace with its labyrinth of rooms housing everything from ancient coats of arms to a vast display of royal jewels, including a stunning eighty-six carat diamond. Luke was particularly amused by the gold- and jewel-encrusted baby crib. The view from the palace gardens was worth the ticket price—a panorama of the Bosphorus Straight busy with freighters and passenger ferries. The courtyard overlooking the water was inlaid with marble, the archways and cozy nooks once meant for royals. The beautiful Iznik tiles were quintessentially Turkish and their vibrant blue, green, and white designs were intricately inlaid throughout the walls and floors. The geometry and patterning of the marble-carved walls and domes begged for a photographer's keen eye, one I wished I had so I could capture the beauty of that place.

As we emerged from the palace gates back into the city center,

Mitch's mobile phone began to buzz. We weren't used to getting texts and calls on a regular basis, preferring to check in with family at a pre-determined time that was convenient for our time zone differences. But suddenly text messages were popping up from his brother, mother, and father.

Are you okay? Let us know you are alright.

Were you near the bombing? We are watching CNN.

Call us!

As Mitch began asking passersby what was happening, I looked around frantically for any signs of danger or confusion. There were none. People were milling about just as they had been before we entered the palace. There were no sirens or helicopters indicating trouble. Even the policemen stationed within view looked calm and relaxed, carrying on as before.

"There was a bombing across the waterway in the Taksim neighborhood," a friendly man offered. "Apparently it was on the main shopping street."

My insides churned as I clutched Luke and thanked God we were okay. We were standing in the shadows of Istanbul's premiere tourist sites and suddenly no amount of police presence made me feel safe. We quickly started walking back to our apartment while Mitch called his family back and reassured them of our safety. We were grateful for social media when a quick Facebook post could alert our friends and extended family following our journey that we were not involved in what they were seeing and hearing on the news. We were close, and I was ready to put some distance between us and the threats of more danger.

With only a day left in our apartment in Istanbul, we decided to explore beyond the city center and took a ferry out to Buyukada, one of the outlying Princes Islands. It was over an hour on the public ferry, which was a breath of fresh air for all of us, particularly our vehicle-loving son. The island boasts bicycles and horse-drawn carriages as its only forms of transportation, so we rented bikes and circumnavigated the island catching seaside views from the hilltops.

On the ferry ride home, Luke laid his head on my lap and napped while the ocean breeze cooled us on the open deck. I looked around at the passengers, most of whom seemed to be locals, and I realized we were sitting alongside families who live and raise their children in this city. They want the same things we do. They want peace and happiness. And I wanted it for them. No one deserves to live in fear of terror in their own backyard. We all want our children to see the best of the world and the people living in it, not the worst.

We were glad to visit Turkey and experience a culture much different than our own. I loved getting to know Istanbul, but I was thankful our next destination was off the beaten path and felt out of harm's way.

TRIP TIP: Istanbul's Museum Pass is a great value if you plan to visit Hagia Sophia and Topkapi Palace. The Pass includes ten other museums (we enjoyed the History of Science and Technology and Mosaic Museums) and pays for itself if you visit just three. You can also avoid ticket queues with your Pass. Children under twelve enter museums for free and don't need a Pass, but we found the adult price well worth it.

16

Cappadocia and the Turkish Coast: Walking through History

I immediately felt my pulse slow to a steady pace again when we arrived in the breathtaking region of Cappadocia. The remote fairyland landscape in the center of Turkey was the perfect antidote to our uneasiness in the city. With outdoor excursions, enticing food, and interesting history, the spectacular setting felt far from modern civilization.

We made the small village of Göreme our home base and checked into Divan Cave House, providing posh cave comfort and wondrous views of the surrounding rock formations that made the area famous. More than 1,000 years ago, early Christian inhabitants carved into the volcanic rock to build homes, churches, and entire communities to escape persecution. I felt like we were re-enacting a bit of their escape as we offloaded our bags in our room and explored the tiny town center for a light lunch. Göreme had the charm of a United States ski town like Breckenridge or Vail with beautiful landscapes and lots of outdoor activities—a whitewashed rural village meant for tourists but maintaining a unique and authentic vibe.

A hot air balloon ride is the quintessential Cappadocian excursion that lives up to all the hype. Photos of sky high, colorful balloons over the iconic hills have launched thousands of Pinterest pins and enviable Instagram posts. It was number one on our wish list.

Our alarm jolted us from a literal hibernation in our cave room at 4:45 a.m., a wakeup call that ended in disappointment when we arrived to find out that it was too windy to send up the balloons that day. On our second attempt, again at 4:45 a.m. the *next* day, it was well worth the wait and we were thrilled to get the green light for liftoff.

The views from above were like nothing we had ever seen before, something like the steep, striped rock layers of the Grand Canyon or Utah's national parks. White rippled volcanic stone and fairy chimneys popped up in bunches out of the ground like thirty-foot birthday candles. We rode high and low for about an hour before landing in a nearby field greeted by friendly employees with champagne, fruit, and certificates of achievement. It was worth every penny—one of the splurges that cannot be missed even when traveling on a tight budget.

When our first attempted balloon ride was cancelled, we didn't have to look far for something else to fill our day. At a nearby all-terrain vehicle rental outfit, we hired a guide who took us through hills, valleys, and even an ancient town carved into a mountain. This was Luke's favorite activity and he drove like a champ, his jet ski experience at my parent's lake house providing training at an early age! After the excursion, Luke was convinced that he would return to Göreme in college to spend a summer working at the ATV outfit giving tours. The off-road adventure through bumpy, dusty roads was a perfect way to view Cappadocia's mountains and fairy chimneys up close.

We also took to the hills on mountain bikes, a more technical adventure through rock caves and steep single tracks. Our cycling friends would be proud of our attempt. We navigated the narrow trails up into the ancient villages for a closer look, exploring a church dating back a millennium where Christians lived and subsequently hid during periods of oppression. Painted frescoes still remain on the ceilings.

We regretted booking our flights for only a three-day stay once we realized how much there was to do in Göreme. One afternoon we took a local bus to nearby Üchasir to explore the historic rock castle and hike Pigeon Valley, but we got sidetracked in a local winery with an employee who poured generously and gave us a complete history of the region's viticulture while we sipped and listened.

We enjoyed every meal, especially after all of the physical activity. For dinner each night, we tucked into a mixed *meze* platter, grilled vegetables, and *döner* wraps with succulent lamb. Lounging on Turkish cushions and sampling the local fare as the sun set in glorious shades across the Rose Valley, we felt a thousand miles away from the rest of the world.

We fell in love with the wonder and magic of Turkey's famed Cappadocia region, and when we set our alarms the last night for an early departure flight, we didn't really want to leave. Funnily enough, we almost didn't have a chance! Unbeknownst to us, Daylight Savings Time started that night and what was supposed to be a 4:30 a.m. wake-up call turned out to be an hour late. We missed our shuttle bus to the airport and had to pay quadruple the amount for a lead-foot taxi driver. He got us to the airport just in the nick of time, but it was an expensive snafu. We had not had many, so we chalked it up to those added expenses that sneak up when you least expect them.

There are many options when deciding where to explore the Turkish coast and we had a hard time narrowing them down. Because we were there in the shoulder season of April instead of summer, the crowds were small and we rented an Airbnb apartment overlooking the water in the quaint seaside town of Bodrum. The highlight of the town for us was the castle, perched high on a hill at the edge of the water keeping watch over the harbor below. The Museum of Underwater Archaeology was housed inside the castle, a fascinating exploration of shipwrecks resurrected from the bottom of the Aegean Sea. The largest museum of its kind, we spent hours marveling at the ancient glass, bronze, and clay items that had been discovered and excavated from the deep waters beneath.

Bodrum also boasts many Roman ruin sites, including a large amphitheater overlooking the sea and a mausoleum that was one of the seven ancient wonders of the world—now just a pile of rubble in an obscure neighborhood. We strolled along the promenades closer to town, watching the seamen clean and repair their boats in anticipation of the coming crowds in the high season. Ironically, one of the most beautiful views along the water was from our table at the local Starbucks! Sometimes a little bit of home in a foreign place is not a bad thing.

After a few nights in Bodrum, we caught the public bus and took it a few hours north to Selçuk, the modern town nearest to the ruins of ancient Ephesus. We booked into a beautiful little family-run place called Hotel Nilya. After quick stops in Cappadocia and Bodrum, we were slowing down in Selçuk for seven nights, and I couldn't be happier with the spot we had chosen.

With beautiful mountain views and the sea just off in the distance, we made ourselves at home in our cozy and affordable suite enjoying the outdoor porch off our room as an extension of our space. We were one of only a few guests and quickly got to know the owners at our daily breakfast in their small dining room. The hotel was crafted with dark, inlaid wood carvings, beautiful glass lanterns, and colorful Turkish tiles on the floors and the walls. Covered balconies and walkways were lush with flowering vines and we spent evenings around the outdoor fire pit learning how to play backgammon, a traditional Turkish game.

One of my personal goals of the trip was achieved while we were in Selçuk. I had mentally collected travel tips and observations from the previous months and penned an article about how to travel internationally with children. I reached out to several publications and, to my surprise, *Huffington Post* expressed interest in my work. They asked me to become a regular blogger on the Family pages of their website, and I found a new hobby in sharing our travel experiences and recommendations.

Within walking distance from our hotel was a surprising site that opened my eyes to the rich Christian history of the region. The ruins of St. John's Basilica sat high on the hill overlooking Selçuk and Ephesus. It is said that John, one of Jesus' disciples, wrote his eponymous book of the Bible while residing there. He spent his later years in that region with Mary, Jesus' mother, whom he promised Jesus he would look after. John is said to be buried on the very site where we were standing, and as we walked among what remained of the columns and archways, I marveled at what a remarkable spot in history this was for me. The book of John is one that I have read and re-read—it is often what I recommend to friends and young mentees who are just beginning to study the Bible. I had never sought out a journey of Christian history but suddenly it found me, and I was struck by the significance of this spot and that we had chosen a hotel within its view.

Ephesus is known for its amazing ruins and was at one time second only in population to Rome itself. One now must imagine the quiet and deserted area once teeming with scholars, merchants, athletes, and 250,000 other inhabitants. Many tourists, including us, came to appreciate the architecture and remains of Roman buildings as thoroughly modern as a library, baths, public toilets, and a theater.

I also continued reveling in the footsteps of early Christian missionaries like Paul and Timothy who walked these streets and began a revolution of belief that would spread around the world. From Paul and Timothy's letters, we know that many aspects of life in Ephesus were not much different from our modern world. The people faced similar problems and temptations, and the apostles' teachings to early followers still bring me hope and encouragement today. Standing amid the beautiful ruins, I straddled ancient and modern times simultaneously.

Mitch, Luke, and I spent several hours listening to Rick Steves' audio walking tour and captured every detail of the excavated remains. The visit solidified my love of Turkey for its diverse history and beauty that I never knew existed. Inhabited by throngs of significant empires from Alexander the Great to the Greeks, Romans, and Turks, the country owns layer upon layer of stories we read in history books. But they come to life when you trod the dirt pathways and breathe it into your soul.

TRIP TIP: We love Rick Steves' website for watching travel videos and reading articles on how to get beyond the tourist sites and have local experiences. Download his Audio Europe app for podcasts and free audio walking tours.

17

Croatia: Easier but Harder

"Mom, why are you and Dad always getting upset with me?"

An innocent question from my son that required a thoughtful answer, and one I wasn't ready to address at 10:00 p.m. after a full day of traveling to a new country.

"Buddy, I'm sorry we get impatient with you. I'm really trying not to get angry. Your constant questions and chatter are exhausting and right now, we need to go to bed."

This was only partly the truth, but I didn't have the strength to expound on the growing frustration I had felt over the last months. I had not had a break from our beloved child who talks constantly—asking a myriad of questions that range from thoughtful to completely off-the-wall. The mental clarity required to respond and engage in his detailed conversations had slowly worn down Mitch and me. We were see-sawing between the snappy, impatient parents we often whispered about and weary wine drinkers before an appropriate hour.

Most days began with positive thoughts from all three of us collaborating on our itinerary and talking over breakfast about what we would learn and experience over the course of the day. Mitch and I could face the day of questions and chatter from our precocious son by tackling it together as a team. By day's end we were tired, but not defeated. Inevitably, though, if the morning began with the necessary schoolwork that physically and mentally weighed us down, Luke would start whining and the suppressed tyrant within me would begin to bellow.

What usually ensued was a toxic cocktail of bribery, threats, and pleading. I was woefully aware of my shortcomings as a teacher, and I am ever so grateful for teachers who devote their life's work to educating our children. I didn't even have to complete much instruction with Luke because he was quick to learn on his own. But the challenge of inspiring him to sit down and do the work without dawdling or staring into space challenged me to my very core. We began those days already depleted and many times it would be difficult to recover.

This internal tension between being responsible, engaging parents and building up the self-confidence of our son became our biggest hurdle as we entered Croatia. Our comfort zone was no longer being stretched by outside influences, but instead by our internal family dynamics. We entered Europe with a sense of accomplishment, feeling at home in the culture and environment and enjoying a bit of celebration and recognition that we had conquered the unknown. But our son was fraying our nerves and we had to dig deep within our relationship, leaning on each other and God for encouragement, patience, and clarity to continue.

We arrived in the capital city of Zagreb anticipating a month of exploration in a country we had wanted to visit for many years. While living in London, many friends extolled the beauty and relatively untouched and little-visited Dalmatian coastline across the Adriatic Sea from Italy. The emerging democracy (following a civil war twenty years' prior) flourished after joining the European Union. Croatia seemed to have all of the benefits of modern Europe with fewer tourists, a better currency exchange, and unspoiled charm.

We checked into the first of many spectacular Airbnb apartments we would find in Croatia, never paying more than $50 USD per night for roomy one- or two-bedroom flats in convenient, walkable neighborhoods. We stuck to our tried-and-true format of introduction to a city and joined a free walking tour of downtown historic Zagreb on our first day.

The capital is known for its laid-back café culture. It is a University town and as our tour guide told us, most people don't work. They are too young, too old, or students. And when you grab a cup of coffee with friends in one of the hundreds of outdoor cafés, you are expected to sit there at least an hour—usually two or three! During the morning, we saw the city's highlights and enjoyed the sunny outdoor offerings along the café-centric Tkalciceva Street under the impressive Zagreb Cathedral's shadow.

"Look guys! An Auto Show!" Luke spotted a billboard in English that beckoned his attention and seemed to be the most compelling thing he had witnessed all morning. "Can we go?"

"Well, it looks like it runs all week, so I think we can go check it out," Mitch replied after checking the details on his phone. "Mom, I think you deserve a day off. Why don't I take Luke for the day tomorrow?"

It was sweet music to my ears. Although we had tag-teamed our parenting responsibility over the past several months, I was more than ready for a quiet afternoon to myself. I had spotted a hair salon down the street from our apartment that was beckoning me and my scraggly, overgrown mane.

"As long as you promise that I can repay the favor next week," I answered. "Let's take turns having a little alone time."

When we are at home in the United States, Mitch and I love to have date nights. We have a steady stream of babysitters who have given us respite on a regular basis since Luke was born. We found the time together rejuvenating, especially in the early years when Mitch traveled for work every week and I was a stay-at-home mother. The quality time kept our marriage and our friendship strong, and sadly it had not yet been possible on our current journey. Time alone would have to suffice until we could get some adult time together.

I made the most of my quiet seven hours. My first stop was the

Tony and Guy hair salon to make an early afternoon appointment, and then I retraced our steps to the busy café district downtown. An outdoor farmers market was in full swing and I slowly perused the carts, picking up small bags of cherries and strawberries to snack on and fresh herbs and carrots to accompany our planned roast chicken dinner.

Although not a coffee drinker, I couldn't miss an opportunity to join the café culture and sip a cup of hot tea while reading a book and writing in my journal. After an hour, I window-shopped back toward my hair appointment and settled into the salon chair under the hands of a friendly Croatian girl who spoke little English, pantomiming gestures of how I would like my hair to be trimmed and shaped.

Mitch and Luke bounded joyfully into the apartment later that evening full of stories and details of every vehicle they witnessed, climbed into, and test drove. They saw hybrid, electric test cars, tractor trailers, and sports cars. It was a boy's dream day out and a mother's gift not to have to endure. I was so grateful for my husband who recognized my need for solitude and his sacrificial heart for allowing me to take my "day off" first.

We thoroughly enjoyed our stop in Zagreb, but if you are visiting Croatia for less than two weeks I would not recommend it as a must-see destination. The culture and Old Town ambience are inviting, but not as intriguing as everything we later encountered. If you are flying in or out of Zagreb, it is worth a day of exploration. And if you are staying more than two weeks in Croatia, I think it is worth a stop.

Our plan to navigate the long and narrow country from top to bottom required a small detour to visit the peninsula of Istria. If you want to experience what coastal and central Italy were probably like before the tourists found them, visit Istria and stay in the seaside town of Rovinj. The northwest region of Croatia has a heavy Italian influence because of its proximity. The food, architecture, and even Italian language are all prominent and we immediately fell in love with the gorgeous blue sea and old, working harbor filled with small fishing boats. The cobblestone streets and quiet alleys are reminiscent of Tuscany; the crumbling stone walls and peeling, painted shutters evoke a period of Renaissance instead of modernity. I became obsessed with photographing the various colors and shapes of the windows and shutters opening out onto the piazza, catching glimpses of old ladies hanging their laundry on the lines high above.

The rocky shore and sea wall bracing the town against the water was the perfect spot for sunset picnics, and we climbed out to find a flat surface several nights in a row with our wine, cheese, and prosciutto to watch the sun go down across the Adriatic Sea. We appreciated Croatia's slow pace and we embraced the culture and lifestyle wholeheartedly.

Beyond the seafood prevalent on menus in Rovinj, we learned about the luxurious Italian-influenced food and wine that came from hill towns just inland. Following Rick Steves' itinerary on a day drive, we stopped in several hilltop villages and small wineries to taste their local grapes and savor the luxurious truffles that make the region famous. Not being a connoisseur of truffles myself, we relied on the proud and kind merchants to educate us on the precise discovery of the delicacy. Dogs root them out of the forest floor during a certain time of year, and because of their notability, the fungi are worth hundreds of dollars per gram.

American chef, author, and TV personality Anthony Bourdain visited the Istrian peninsula on one of his shows, "No Reservations." We had already followed his recommendations in Vietnam and Cambodia and now relied on the YouTube episodes as we traveled to uncover adventurous food experiences. He directed us to the town of Motovun, high upon a hill that was a strain on our small hatchback followed by a steep walk into the pedestrian-only town center. Our destination was Mondo Konoba, a small establishment built into the hillside with generations of truffle-laden recipes and traditions under its belt. After several stops at local wineries, Mitch and I had developed an appetite and the luxurious, potent fragrance wafting from the kitchen summoned us.

"What are your specialties?" Mitch asked our friendly waiter as he eyed the selections, each boasting truffles as the highlight. We were seated on their outdoor porch overlooking the valley below. A bottle of wine had been poured and a perfect evening was poised to take place.

"The homemade pasta ribbons with shaved truffles and butter sauce is always a favorite," the server offered. "You will also like the omelet with truffles—a very light but decadent dish."

How could we choose? Everything looked divine. After many nights of picnic suppers or basic meals in the apartment, even the simplest dish looked elaborate and tempting to my growling stomach.

"I think we'll have the pasta with truffles, the filet of steak with truffles, and the bread with black olive and truffle tapenade," Mitch announced.

"Excellent choices, sir. I'll bring the warm bread now."

Luke must have sensed that Mitch and I were trying to create a romantic evening with him in tow because he quietly read his book during the entire evening stopping only to comment positively on his pasta with truffles, a luxury I'm not sure many eight year olds get to experience. Mitch and I devoured our shared dishes, appreciating the special meal and our surroundings with full hearts of gratitude. These were the nights I would remember—not the wearied and impatient times when we wondered how we could keep our wits about us—but the moments that were completely full of new and beautiful smells, tastes, and sights.

Istria embedded itself in our hearts and before we began the trek south on the Croatian coast, we visited Mondo Konoba again for one last exquisite truffle meal. We enjoyed several days riding bikes for miles along the seaside promenade and day-tripping to the nearby port town of Pula and the fashionable, nineteenth-century resort town, Opatija.

Croatia is very diverse given its small size. Navigating the country in our rental car was easy, and in just a few hours we went from coastal, Italian-like Istria to mountainous, Austro-Hungarian Northern Dalmatia. We stopped just outside Plitvice National Park, known for its waterfalls. The remote inland area only warranted one night's stay, but a full day hiking in the fresh air of the park under the vast and numerous waterfalls was glorious.

From Plitvice we skirted back out toward the coast to historic Split where we stayed in another one of our many favorite Airbnb apartments. It was a second-story walk-up with modern furnishings for only $40 USD per night with a kind and enthusiastic hostess who epitomized the Croatian friendliness we felt across the country. Croatia was proving to have all the European culture and charm, but none of the tourists and a fraction of the price. Visiting in the shoulder season of April was helpful, but I don't believe the crowds are ever as suffocating as what you find in Rome or Florence's high season.

Split is the gateway to Croatia's 2,000 islands and we intended to visit a few. The ferries are plentiful and run regularly to the outlying islands. We decided to visit the island of Brac, known for its beaches. To save a few dollars, we opted to ride the ferry without our car and took the public bus to the nearby town of Bol. We spent the afternoon on the locally-famous beach of Zlatne Rad and marveled at the crystal blue water alongside other families enjoying an easy-going afternoon at the seaside.

Split offered many of our recently-discovered past times and we spent several afternoons riding bicycles in a large, waterfront park. We visited the Maritime Museum which was chocked full of torpedoes because the inventor was from Croatia. Luke even managed to spot an advertised boat show and we spent the afternoon wandering the docks and climbing on vessels of all sizes.

Diocletian's Palace remains are in the center of the historic pedestrian district. We lost ourselves among the many tiny alleys within the old palace walls. Climbing to the top of the marble bell tower, we saw views of the red tiled rooftops just beneath us and the green forested hills in the distance. Across an entire side, we were surrounded by the turquoise waters that buffeted the town.

With a farmer's market nearby and no fastidious itinerary, we enjoyed living simply, intermingling with locals and wondering how much more chaotic this port town becomes in the heat of the summer.

We decided to take our next island excursion in our rental car and drove it onto the ferry early one morning. Luke excitedly watched as the winding snake of vehicles efficiently stacked themselves into the bowels of the boat. We exited the car and found our seats on the top deck for the three-hour journey to Korcula.

Korcula boasts a magnificent, historic Old Town—a small peninsula at the water's edge laid out with a main street and parallel side streets off either side. Looking at it from above, the layout of the town resembles a fish skeleton. The design was intended to reduce the effects of the wind and provides citizens with shade as they navigate the tiny streets. The medieval towers and walls fortifying its harbor beckon tourists, but it was quiet and serene when we arrived.

Checking into our apartment, we agreed that staying a few minutes outside of historic town centers was better for our budget and usually offered a free place to park our car. When we stepped onto our porch and saw the stunning waterfront views and rooftops of the Old Town, we confirmed our strategy and recommend it to fellow budget travelers.

The car was necessary to explore the entire island. We discovered inland hill towns with wineries and secluded coves with smooth-pebbled beaches and the odd fisherman bobbing in his boat. I was struck at how quiet and undiscovered the country was compared to its nearby European neighbors. I loved the thrill of discovering these seemingly untouched areas. There were no large tour buses or crowded streets and restaurants, and the people we met were incredibly friendly. While having lunch in a small town, we met a local man running errands who invited us to follow him to his house to try his wine. We accepted his generous invitation and had a fabulous afternoon learning about his family, his boutique winery, and his enviable view over the harbor. We were doing our best to integrate into a local environment without being noticed and got a glimpse behind the curtains of what life was like in these beautiful spots around the world.

Throughout our time in Croatia, Mitch and I were remembering and re-learning the recent past of former Yugoslavia and the complicated history of its civil war in the 1990's. Just as I felt in Cambodia, I was embarrassed and ashamed that I only had vague memories of the atrocities mentioned on the nightly news. I was in high school in America focused only on the world I could see around me.

We spent many nights after Luke went to bed watching documentaries of the war and ethnic cleansing among the Croats, Bosnians, and Serbs. I still don't fully understand it, but we grew in our desire to know more about the region's marked history and how the aftermath affected the lives of people we were meeting. After leaving Split, instead of continuing down the coast of Croatia, we made a sharp turn north into Bosnia to explore Mostar and Sarajevo.

TRIP TIP: If you love exploring a country's food culture, it's fun to follow Anthony Bourdain and his adventures around the world. We always researched his recommendations on episodes of "No Reservations" and "Parts Unknown" on YouTube before starting in a new country that he had visited.

18

Bosnia: Understanding the Atrocities

Driving away from the beauty of the coast, we immediately felt we were entering a more rural, Communist-era country. Bosnia and Herzegovina (as it is officially known) has not recovered from the war as well as Croatia, and we passed building after building either bombed out or riddled with bullet holes.

The town of Mostar is small but significant—a village deep in the Mostar River valley between two steep mountain ranges above. The famous Stari Most bridge, beautifully arched over the rushing water far below, physically connected the divide of Croats and Bosniaks (Bosnian Muslims), but during the bloody war it was demolished. Countrymen and neighbors fought against each other—a complex and senseless war. As we walked the streets, we could still see pock-marked buildings that had never been restored or reclaimed, a harrowing reminder of the past. Death was still fresh as we walked through the park-turned-cemetery where every grave was dated 1993, 1994, or 1995.

With the reconstruction of the bridge in recent years, a revitalization came to the town. Now it stands as a reminder of history and a symbol of reconnection after a dark period of divide. Despite our rainy afternoon there, we were among many other tourists walking through town soaking in the combined beauty and tragic history. I was struck by the resilience and recovery of these people—the younger generation striving to work together for a more productive and inclusive future.

Why must we be divided? It happens so often, not just in Bosnia, but in my own country half a world away. Political differences, racial divide—they threaten to tear us apart. Witnessing the aftermath that is still evident after more than twenty years in Bosnia, it was heartbreaking and frustrating to me that humanity continued to live in discord instead of peace in many places around the world.

My discomfort and sadness weighed on me. But I'm glad it did and I let it simmer throughout our visit to Bosnia. Seeing firsthand what can happen to a society that tears each other apart instead of living in peaceful acceptance of one another's differences left a mark on my heart and a staid determination to love and respect my neighbors.

Further north toward Sarajevo, we were greeted with snowflakes as Old Man Winter put a stop to our summer chase.

"SNOW!" Luke bellowed from the backseat as we climbed the mountains into the white-out on the winding road from Mostar. The rain in the valley had turned to thick, wet accumulation as we reached the higher elevation. Luke was elated.

"Let's make some snowballs, Dad! And a snowman!"

"Well, I'm not sure there's enough for a snowman, but we can pull over and check it out," Mitch relented.

We pulled off the highway and created a roadside snowball fight in the hills of Bosnia, freezing our digits and realizing quickly we were not dressed appropriately to be out in the elements. It was certainly a fun memory and my child who rarely sees any snow living in the southern United States got to catch large, wet snowflakes on his tongue and leave his footprints on the Balkan mountainside that afternoon.

The snow continued and eventually turned to slush as we descended into the valley of Sarajevo. The next morning was sunny but cold and we bundled up to join a free walking tour of the city. I was particularly interested in hearing firsthand about the siege of the city during the war and learn how the city and its people had recovered. I had no idea how impactful the morning would be, encountering a child survivor of the war.

Neno was seven years old and living in an apartment with his parents when the siege on Sarajevo began. His father went off to war and his mother, determined to support her family and rebuke the enemy firing down from the mountaintops, continued walking to work every day. The school closed from fear for the children's safety, so the children in Neno's apartment began meeting in the basement under the guidance of a young teacher who also lived there. Soon the families would have to live in the basement to avoid the constant barrage of sniper fire. For four long years, Neno lived in the bowels of the building burning furniture to stay warm and seeing sunlight for only twenty minutes each day when his teacher allowed them to stretch their legs and run around the covered courtyard.

Neno is now a tour guide—an ambassador to his beloved Sarajevo. He is the epitome of resilience; speaking softly of his difficult early years but proudly boasting of the modern city and how the citizens are striving to recover and move on. There was a hint of sadness in his voice and in older residents we met in Sarajevo. We heard a caustic, dry sense of humor from years of trying to find the good in a very bleak situation. But Neno's resolve to educate visitors about the past while introducing them to the city's emerging vibrancy was contagious. I found myself extolling the highlights of the city to friends and strangers wanting them to feel the revitalization born out of gut-wrenching pain. Being invited into Neno's story and walking through the tragedy to see the beauty on the other side brought me hope. Experiencing these emotions reminded me why we kept pushing ourselves out of our comfort zone—to learn and empathize with others and appreciate the stories they have to tell.

We re-entered Croatia and spent our last days in Dubrovnik, aptly named the "Pearl of the Adriatic." The sea is so clear we could see straight to the bottom looking down into it from a mountaintop. The shades of turquoise shimmered and competed only in radiance with the enormous, blinding sunlit sky. Rugged mountains layered the ancient city's backdrop, some snow-capped and some peaked with jagged, gray stone and fresh with evergreens below. The beauty, diversity, and history of Dubrovnik were captivating. We strolled the whitewashed stone streets and circumnavigated the ancient city walls for hours soaking in the history as our cool ice cream cones dripped in the warm sun.

The Croatian people, just like the Bosnians, hide a recent painful history behind their smiles and concerted efforts to forge ahead. Witnessing the rebirth of Dubrovnik was proof of the energy and willingness to rebuild after a separate harrowing siege on their beloved old city during the war. We had witnessed the destruction from behind both sides of enemy lines and no one was the victor. If you stopped and looked long enough you could still see sadness in the locals' eyes. It was impossible to ignore. Only the teenagers seemed to have the genuine laugh of a carefree attitude since they didn't bear the scars from twenty years ago.

Just as we arrived in Dubrovnik, I learned of a tragedy back home in Athens. Four college students were killed in a car accident and the driver, a friend and regular visitor to our home, was in critical condition fighting for her life. I was heartbroken by the news, sad to be so far away when I wanted to be comforting my young grieving college friends. As I voraciously read online news coverage and communicated with friends over the coming days, I marveled at the response of our tight-knit community and the hope of hundreds striving to seek a purpose in the unexplainable sadness.

It was another testament to me that our world is broken, but in God we can find peace, comfort, and the will to put one foot in front of the other, never quite understanding why these unspeakable wars and tragedies happen. I was thankful to trust in something bigger than this world, especially when the world looked unrecognizable.

I will always think of my friend Agnes, her bright smile, and her unshakeable faith when I remember Bosnia and Croatia and their complexities in beauty and in brokenness.

TRIP TIP: The drive from Mostar to Sarajevo is beautiful but intense. We recommend traveling during the day and staying alert on the winding mountainous roads. Build in time to travel through the border crossings from Croatia to Bosnia. Since Bosnia is not part of the European Union, be prepared to show your passport as you enter the country.

19

Southern Italy:
Life on the Farm

"We have got to keep pushing ourselves onto the ledge," Mitch confided in me one night. "Otherwise our time in Italy will feel like an extended vacation of beaches and vineyards."

I agreed. Italy held a treasured place in our hearts and we already had many luxurious holidays exploring almost every region. But the purpose of this visit was to learn to live like locals and attempt to soak up their culture and slow-paced lifestyle.

"I'm a city girl through and through, but I do think it would be fun to try out life on a farm," I replied. "It will be a great learning experience for all of us and I know you would enjoy getting your hands dirty."

"I'm ready to sweat—and not just lying on a beach," Mitch grinned.

"Let's find a farm with lots of animals!" Luke piped in. "I'd like to play with some dogs and feed goats and chickens."

"I'll see if I can accommodate that request," I said, smiling at my enthusiastic son. He had never toiled a day in his life so it would be interesting to watch him undertake a little bit of work to earn his keep.

Several months earlier I had begun reading and researching a worldwide trend called WWOOFing, which stands for Willing Workers on Organic Farms. Many countries around the world participate in the volunteer phenomenon for backpackers and serious folks who want to learn how to farm sustainably. We are neither of those but wanted to check it out and dive into an authentic Italian family experience. The idea of working on a farm in exchange for our room and board was intriguing but I wanted to find just the right situation for our family since we were bringing along a child.

Farmsteads offer a range of accommodation options from pitching a tent in the backyard to rooms in their home or a separate garage apartment. Each farm requires a variety of responsibilities depending on what they grow and harvest. While Mitch and I had visions of trimming vineyard vines in a bucolic hillside setting, we knew that Italy had the most competitive opportunities and we would have to search through thousands of volunteer listings before requesting and being accepted by a farmer and his family.

From Dubrovnik we traveled via overnight ferry to the Southern Italian region of Puglia, known for a rich agricultural heritage and slightly grittier, less-refined atmosphere than its northern neighbors. Puglia was a region we had never explored and the lack of tourists and plentiful farming opportunities led us to study the WWOOFing options there. After culling through listings and narrowing down the choices that allowed children, offered a separate sleeping area for a family, and did not require a month-long stay, I reached out to Le Fattizze farm down in the heel of Italy's boot. Through a broken English/Italian conversation over email using Google Translate, I learned we were graciously accepted and the Rolli family eagerly anticipated our arrival at their farm for a week's stay.

The mystery of what we would encounter at Le Fattizze had me restless one night.

"I'm pretty sure they don't speak a lick of English," I told Mitch, lying beside him in a quiet farmhouse outside the Puglian town of Lecce. We had arrived a few days before our scheduled workweek to explore the area and found it to be as charming, authentic, and untouched as we had read.

"Don't worry," Mitch replied with a smile. "They'll show us

what to do and we can practice our Italian." He and I had attempted Italian lessons many years before but I still couldn't form a full sentence when under pressure.

"Besides," he continued, "the whole reason we are doing this is to experience something new and different. It's okay to feel uncomfortable. We know we aren't farmers and that will be hilarious and fun. But we are the kind of people who like to help others, and I'm pretty excited about eating home-cooked Italian meals!"

I could always count on my husband to see the bright side of the challenges set before us, and he never failed to remind me that these conscious decisions we made were all part of our intended adventure.

It's not about me, I reminded myself for what seemed like the thousandth time. *It's about opening myself up to others and being uncomfortable so that I can grow, too.*

The next afternoon, we pulled onto a long dirt road that led to the farm and I braced myself for the unknown. As we exited our car, we were met by a large clan of beaming Italians hugging us and welcoming us to their farm. We reciprocated and thankfully everyone's welcome was universally understood because there was not much deep conversation or understanding after that.

The Rollis are a precious Southern Italian crew—a quintessential, multi-generational family living and working together every day. Papa and Mama come over each morning to the farm where sister and brother, Alice (that's Ah-LEE-chay in Italian!) and Marco, live and run Le Fattizze, an agri-campground. There are many different aspects of the farm that earn the family a modest living. While their main source of income, the gorgeous olive oil, was not being harvested in the season we were there, they had many other jobs that needed our help.

All of my language gap anxieties were laid to rest when we were introduced to the other WWOOFer staying on the property, Diego, whom we dubbed our Argentinean angel. Diego had been volunteering at the farm for several weeks and not only did he speak English, Italian, and Spanish, but he learned his English while living in Roswell, Georgia, as a child—just a few miles from where Mitch and I grew up! Diego served as our translator and became a close friend of Mitch's as they worked side by side on several projects.

Luke was thrilled to see that the Rollis had goats, chickens, rabbits, and a few dogs who followed Papa around faithfully, an Italian version of Old McDonald. The property was also home to a campsite, which we were told was filled to maximum capacity with holiday campers in June, July, and August. Since it was early May, we had the task of cleaning the grounds, picking up litter, and pulling weeds in anticipation of a busy summer around the corner.

Mitch and Diego built a goat shed to protect the mama and her new babies from the intensifying sun. Luke and I gathered eggs each morning and we all helped cook and clean up each night. It was eye opening how easily we fell into a simple daily routine and these strangers quickly became like family. When you sit around a breakfast table with someone, even if you can't speak their language, you begin to know them intimately. We would arrive to the kitchen for breakfast bleary-eyed after a warm night in our rustic room. Alice would always have strong coffee waiting for Mitch, and Luke and I would fill our bellies with homemade scones, bread, and jam made from the *nespola* fruit hanging from the tree outside the window. The Rollis grew a large percentage of the food they ate. There were various fruit trees dotting the property and a large garden that produced greens, fresh tomatoes, and herbs by the bushel every day.

Mama settled herself into the kitchen when we all began our outdoor chores and by lunchtime she created a feast of handmade pasta using fresh eggs from the coop and sauce from vegetables in the garden that we enjoyed on the long outdoor picnic table. The food was unbelievably fresh and flavorful and I snuck in the tiny galley kitchen a few mornings to watch over her shoulder and try to learn her recipes. I'm not sure I could ever duplicate them but I was reminded that cooking was a universal language of love and friendship as we stood quietly cracking eggs and exchanging smiles.

Joining the family meals and experiencing a true Italian table was one of my greatest joys while WWOOFing. The conversation—while stilted in English—was more enjoyable when flowing in Italian among our hosts. We would sit back and listen to the melody, not understanding a single word. Diego and Alice pulled out their guitars after dinner and serenaded us with slow Italian songs; harmonies warmed the small living space. Luke laid his head in my lap and whispered, "I love Italy." I nodded in agreement and said a prayer of thanks for the experience that wove us into the fabric of another family on our journey.

Our week at Le Fattizze, which was meant to push us once again, ended up being a triumph and treasured memory. Don't misunderstand—it was a stretch out of the comfort zone in more ways than one. The mosquitos took their toll on our exposed limbs, I didn't wash my hair for days, and my back ached from a paper-thin mattress and marathon weed-pulling sessions. But those small setbacks were nothing in comparison to the unique experience and heartwarming gift of embracing friendship and family in a country we adore while stepping into their simple and beautiful lives for even just a few days.

TRIP TIP: Willing Workers on Organic Farms is a trusted organization, but it takes serious research to determine the best fit for your family. Since each country requires a paid subscription to gain access to their listings, consider which country in which you might like to volunteer and plan to reach out to many farms before finding the right fit. It's worth the time and effort to ensure a positive experience for you, your family, and your hosts.

20

Sicily: Italy Unvarnished

As children of the 1980's, Mitch and I grew up on movie classics like *ET, The Goonies,* and *Stand by Me.* Mitch's family, however, did not cozy up by the fireplace at Christmastime and watch *A Christmas Story* or *National Lampoon's Christmas Vacation.* No, they popped *The Godfather* into the VCR (nothing like a little bit of mafia and bloody retribution to bring cheer during the holiday season). After those childhood memories, it was understandable that Mitch wanted to visit the Corleone's homeland while we were in Southern Italy. I simply went for the cannoli.

We left Le Fattizze and drove a few hours toward the tip of Italy's boot to cross the short straight to Sicily. Faithfully following Google Maps, Mitch turned sharply left onto a dirt road and we began bumping around in our sedan, wondering if our guide had given us a wrong turn.

"Honey, I think maybe we better turn around," I nudged gently.

"No, this is what the map says," Mitch answered. "Let's go a bit further and see if it pops us back out onto a proper road."

The potholes grew larger and our car's suspension was working overtime when I noticed neat rows of green out of my window.

"Oh no!" I gasped. "We are in a field. Those look like red onions!"

Sure enough, our Google Maps "fail" had sent us straight into a farmer's vast harvest of onions. We started looking frantically for an opportunity to turn around but only saw more narrow rows of stalks and divots for irrigation.

"I'm turning around," Mitch muttered impatiently, throwing the car into reverse. He turned the wheel sharply and pressed into the gas pedal. The car lurched backward and directly into a ditch.

"What happened?!" cried Luke, looking up from his Kindle, oblivious to how we had ended up in this quandary.

"Not a word!" Mitch fumed as he jumped out of the car to assess the damage.

Until then we had been relatively lucky with our rental cars, spending a month in Croatia and Bosnia without a scratch. It seemed our luck had run out.

"The damage is minor but I can't get us out of this ditch," Mitch reported. "I'm going to try and find some help."

In the middle of an onion farm? There were no other cars around (naturally), but as I swiveled my head I caught sight of a large tractor half a mile away working in the field. Mitch walked in that direction and I giggled to myself. We were literally in a rut. How's that for irony?

A few minutes later, Mitch jogged back giving me the thumbs up and behind him I could see the tractor slowly rolling toward our inverted car. A friendly old Italian man came over with a rope and a large hook while Mitch climbed underneath to find a sturdy bar on which to clip it. He jumped back in the driver's seat and started the engine, keeping the five speed in neutral.

"Okay! We are ready!" he shouted out his window to the Good Samaritan behind us.

With a tug and a small pop we began to rise out of the ditch. The damage was minor—a crack on the rear fender—but we were rescued!

"I can't thank you enough for your kindness," Mitch told the farmer, who spoke absolutely no English. "*Grazie mille. Grazie mille.*"

We found the nearest exit lane out of the onions and were

back on the road in less than two minutes, but the aftermath of the morning's excitement stayed with us for many miles. We were so grateful for the helping hands and wondered how else we would have escaped the mess without that kind and generous soul. We had met our second angel in Italy, and as we drove toward the docks to catch our ferry we said another quick prayer of thanks for our good fortune.

We were a little nervous crossing from the tip of Italy's boot over to the eastern seaboard of Europe's largest island. Sicilian stereotypes were set in our minds, and with our nerves a bit frayed from the morning's onion adventure we were on guard for the veritable mobsters and hoodlums that could be lurking around every bend. But it only took a few days cruising the coastline and exploring Sicilian culture to banish our concerns and embrace the unvarnished Italy we discovered.

We had our sights set on the volcanic Mount Etna and settled into an apartment in a tiny, seaside port town near its base. On a clear day the snowy mountaintop could be viewed from fifty miles in any direction. There was often a stream of wispy smoke billowing like a lit cigarette, reminding visitors and residents of the ever-present danger of eruption. Because Europe's tallest active volcano was at rest while we were there, we were able to drive up and explore the craggy, steep craters created from past explosions. It felt other-worldly, like we had landed on another planet. We braced ourselves when we exited the car against the incredible sixty-mile-per-hour winds that threatened to push us off the volcano's edge. I held tightly to Luke as he played astronaut, picking up lava rocks—basalt, obsidian, and pumice—full of holes and history. The most recent eruption had come just months before, thankfully with no destruction to the towns below. But Etna was still very alive with its lava gurgling just below the surface and we could feel the forces of nature battling through earth, wind, and fire.

Second only to the magnificence of Mount Etna was the food in Sicily. Before we even set foot on the island we discovered *arancini*, a volcano-shaped fried finger food consisting of rice and variations of meat, cheese, and vegetables. The metaphor continues as you bite into the top—heat exploding from the surface and savory flavors greeting your taste buds. We tried our first *arancini* on board our ferry, copying all the locals and guessing that it must be good if they were willing to queue up in the ferry's questionable cafeteria. The hearty and handy snack became our go-to meal in every town thereafter, a cheap and delicious taste of Sicily's fast food.

Exploring local town markets was also a great way to grab fast and fresh food and I found the market in Syracuse to be one of my favorites. Lively and bustling with local shoppers and friendly but aggressive street vendors, we walked down the lane and past multiple tents before I could fully take in all the color and smells and actually wrap my brain around which delightful sustenance we would purchase. Luke had become our purveyor, practicing his Italian and charming the men and women alike who were selling their fruits, vegetables, meats, and olives.

"*Vorrei cinquecento gramme, per favore?*" he asked politely, pointing at the strawberries.

"*Bene, bene,*" the kind man replied, bagging the beautiful fruit. Luke grinned.

"See, I think they give you the very best if you try and speak their language," I explained.

Our theory was proven right again and again and soon Luke's vocabulary exploded with the certainty that he was securing us the best food that each vendor had to offer. And it paid off for him at the gelato counter, too. His scoops were always bigger than mine after sweet-talking the employees!

While Luke and Mitch explored the Leonardo da Vinci Invention Museum, I strolled through the piazzas and ruins of Syracuse nibbling on strawberries. Why did I ever worry about coming to this gorgeous part of Italy? My prejudices weighed me down and I scolded myself for believing the stereotypes before I experienced this place for myself. Sicily, and all Southern Italy we had explored on this trip, had everything that I love about Italy and none of what I don't. We had not waited in line once or been crushed by a sea of tourists. The people had been kind and open, willing to listen to our attempts at broken Italian instead of immediately speaking English back to us in frustration of our shortcomings. They seem to be happy we had visited and were proud of their island, its history, and its beauty. And even if none of this had been true, the food alone made Sicily worth a visit.

We were on a steady diet of daily gelato before we entered Sicily and then we added cannoli to our dessert course. In the tiny hilltop town of Noto we discovered what authentic cannoli tastes like. Nothing in the freezer section of American grocery stores would ever come close to this. Recalling the education from our Airbnb host upon arrival, we only ordered cannoli from cafés that did not already have them stuffed and chilling in the refrigerated glass case. The flaky shells must be empty, ready for fresh filling, and made to order. It was clearly an art form enjoying these decadent desserts.

As the barista prepared Mitch's espresso, I watched his colleague pipe the white, creamy ricotta mixture into a small fried pastry tube. I could barely get out of the café before I had to take a bite of the cold, crunchy, and creamy decadence. It was like tasting heaven in three short bites. It was gone too soon but there would be more in my future. Instinctively I knew, like the best gelato, these little treats could not be easily replicated back home so we indulged daily while we were visiting their place of origin.

We continued to circumnavigate Sicily and landed in the quaint beach town of Cefalù. Luke was ready to run and play in the sand and Mitch and I agreed a few days lying in the sun would be the revitalizing break we needed before the next month of travel. We were picking up our pace, visiting four countries over the next four weeks, and welcoming visitors. A few quiet days on the beach would set our minds straight for the busy weeks ahead.

Cefalù offers the longest stretch of sand on the island so it's considerably busy with sun worshippers, families building castles, and children jumping the Tyrrhenian sea waves as they crash on the white sandy shore. Besides the beach, Cefalù's medieval town center is postcard-perfect with windy, narrow lanes and a soaring cathedral in the town's main square. After a full day in the sun we fell into the Italian routine of an evening passeggiata—a slow stroll through the streets—winding up at the edge of the water to watch another sunset.

On a Sunday morning, I requested that we go to church to admire the inside of the cathedral and lift another prayer for our recovering friend, Agnes. We knew the service would be spoken in Italian, so when Luke started squirming impatiently in the wooden pew, the boys snuck out and I remained. Opening my Bible on my e-reader, I turned to the New Testament and began reading the book of John—praying, meditating, and listening to the rhythmic sounds of the service going on around me. I looked up, and towering above the congregation in the dome of the apse was a beautiful, imposing mosaic of Christ brilliantly shimmering in flecks of gold and blue.

In those moments of reflection, God spoke clearly to me about being present with Him in each moment. I had been challenging myself the entire trip to live in the moment and enjoy each breath and experience we encountered. He was reminding me to not just *be*, but *be with Him*. He reminded me not to worry about the impending visits from family and not to be anxious about planning for the future, something I had begun rolling over in my mind as our travel days grew to a close on our last continent. Staring up at the loving eyes of my Lord in that ancient church, I was comforted in knowing that God had already laid our future out for us—and it was good. His plans are bigger than my plans; His thoughts are greater than my thoughts.

But, what are they? I wondered silently. *What are those plans?*

We had chosen to give God our whole lives, not just this adventure. As long as our fate and our future were in His hands I had to have faith, listen, and trust that He would direct our paths. Where He leads, I will follow.

Our final Sicilian days were spent in Palermo, the gritty city that—after the likes of India and Bangkok—did not seem so intimidating. It felt very urban hipster, a Mediterranean version of Brooklyn. The food tour continued as we branched out into daring delicacies: spleen sandwiches, roasted eggplant, and *frito misto*—a fried mix of indeterminable seafood, capped off naturally by gelato and cannoli. The city grew louder and more vibrant as the darkness of night settled in, but instead of joining the throngs on the streets we cozied up in our studio apartment for a good night's sleep before our marathon transpired the following day.

TRIP TIP: While we didn't meet any Sicilian mobsters, it is still wise to use street smarts in Sicily—or any other foreign country for that matter. When you park your rental car, choose a busy area and do not leave any items in view. Check the ground in the parking lot. If there are glass shards from broken windshields, find a different area to leave your vehicle.

21

Spain, Italy, and France:
Field Trips and Family

We traded in our slow pace of travel for fast and furious field trips in Italy and Spain. Luke requested that we visit Barcelona since he was learning Spanish at school before we left. His teacher studied abroad there and while teaching her students the language she also lauded Barcelona's delicious food and quirky architecture. Mitch and I loved the Spanish port city and decided it was a worthwhile detour.

When researching the flights from Palermo it seemed inevitable that we would have a layover, so Mitch cleverly booked us tickets with a twelve-hour stop in Rome. The detour en route to the detour would be another fun and educational stop for Luke since he had never seen the Coliseum but wanted to add it to his repertoire of Roman ruins. Thus we began our frenzied week of sightseeing, plunging into mainland Europe at the cusp of high season.

After landing at Rome's Leonardo da Vinci Airport, we quickly boarded a bus designed for tourists like us who had only a few hours to get to the city center and witness a few sights before the next leg of their flight. The bus dropped us off in town and we bee-lined into the first pizzeria we found, grabbing three enormous slices and a big bottle of water to sustain us through the afternoon. There was no time for leisurely lunches or café coffee stops. We were hustling—a complete departure from our usual pace.

Mitch and I had been to Rome on our honeymoon and decided

it was more economical for one of us to take Luke into the Coliseum rather than pay for three tickets. Happy for some alone time, I offered to stay outside and spent a few hours reading with the crumbling structure towering above me.

Using the Rick Steves' Audio Europe app, the boys listened and learned about the ancient playground for Romans while tethered together by Mitch's phone, two sets of ear buds, and a splitter (a travel necessity for couples and families). Luke was impressed by the stories of brave gladiators fighting to the death and, being a fourth-generation engineer, Mitch enjoyed the architectural wonder of Roman engineering.

When they emerged from the stadium we briskly walked down via dei Fori Imperiali toward the iconic Trevi Fountain. Luke made a wish as he threw his coin into the water and then we rushed to the Pantheon, a circular temple-turned-church with a breathtaking opening in the center of the domed ceiling leading up to God.

I feared the final two monuments were lost on Luke as the heat of the day sapped our energy and tourists crushed us from every side.

"Yikes! We've got to get going!" Mitch shouted, looking at his watch. We had been loitering inside the cool, dark Pantheon and didn't realize our bus back to the airport was departing in less than fifteen minutes. We were more than a mile away.

"Alright buddy, strap on your running shoes!" I said encouragingly to Luke. He looked less than pleased.

We jogged through the crowds and navigated the busy streets while keeping our patience with Luke, who was lagging behind. After all, it wasn't his fault that his parents overestimated our afternoon and couldn't help but pack as much as possible into our Roman holiday.

Sweaty and breathless, we arrived too late. The bus had departed minutes earlier, but thankfully the next one on the route was ready and waiting for us—an air-conditioned respite for our tired legs. We had showed Rome to Luke but we would have to come back and do it properly the next time.

Our plane took off from Italy again, and as I watched the city shrink beneath us, I was thankful it wasn't my last glimpse of the country. We would be back, albeit in a different region, in a few short weeks with my brother-in-law and niece.

The flight to Barcelona was short but the sun had long since set by the time we emerged from El Prat Airport exhausted, sticky from the humidity, and hungry. Our pizza from twelve hours earlier had long since digested. We hopped aboard the public bus that took us into the city center where we boarded the underground metro for several stops. Finally, we began walking the long mile toward our hotel. For only three Euros it was more economical than a taxi, but I was ready for a shower, a meal, and my bed. It was midnight and we were all falling apart.

"I'm so hungry and my feet hurt!" cried Luke, dragging his suitcase listlessly down the deserted sidewalk. I really empathized with him. I was drained, too. We had been moving at a hare's pace since 6:00 a.m.

It must be noted that Luke was a total trooper 99 percent of the journey. The child is not one for meltdowns, a quality I deeply admire and appreciate when I know he's tired and we have stretched him beyond his limit. I could usually offer a pep talk when we arrived late at night into a new country. That would usually summon a second (or third) burst of energy from him and we could make it to our destination with everyone's wits intact. But tonight we were losing him quickly and I looked to Mitch for moral support.

"Hey, Mitch. Isn't that a McDonald's up ahead?" I winked and silently hoped he would pick up on my fake, cheerful cadence.

"Why, yes it is!" he replied, my quick witted co-host of this late night sketch.

"How about we let Dad get us some Mickey D's while we shower and get in our jammies?" I offered Luke, whose eyes were beginning to sparkle again. "I bet they'll even have ice cream."

Sold. Luke picked up his pace and we waved Mitch off as he crossed the street to pick up an unhealthy and totally American fast food dinner. Our Barcelona sangria and tapas meals would have to wait.

With only three days in Barcelona we decided to join the free walking tour that showed off architect Antonio Gaudi's famous buildings. His colorful and fluid designs have marked the city since the early twentieth century and the still-unfinished masterpiece, La Sagrada Familia, is an icon towering over the perpetually-sunny Mediterranean city.

Luke had communicated with his second-grade class a few times on our journey, thanks to his loyal teacher and the modern technology of FaceTime. It had been several months since his update to the class on elephants so we thought it was a great time to tell his classmates firsthand about Barcelona.

"Hola!" Luke hollered when he saw his friends on the computer screen. He rarely got homesick but seeing their sweet faces even made me tear up.

"Guess where I am, guys?" he asked their inquisitive faces. "Barcelona!"

"Luke, tell the class about La Sagrada Familia!" Ms. Billmayer prompted. "Is it as big as it looks in pictures?"

"Yes, even bigger," Luke replied. "The outside still isn't finished, but the inside columns look like trees holding up the high ceiling. It's really amazing!"

My chest burst with pride as I watched Luke engage with his peers, enthusiastic about what he had learned. He seemed well aware of the opportunity he had been given to experience these iconic world monuments and pieces of history in person instead of reading about them in a book.

"Guess what we ate last night? McDonald's!"

My pride quickly turned to mortification. The *one* American fast food meal we had eaten in six months was now the highlight of Luke's Spanish presentation. My second grader was keeping it real for his followers at home, that's for sure.

His teacher passed her phone around the room so each child

could ask Luke a specific question. They ranged from general to obscure—each sweet friend genuinely interested in what he was seeing and experiencing. I was grateful these little ones had not forgotten about him in his absence. I was reassured that going home, for Luke at least, might be an easy transition back into his former life.

Barcelona has some of the best food in Europe, in my opinion, so we strolled through the Boqueria Market sampling cured meats, cheeses, and fruit every afternoon. Since the locals don't eat dinner until nearly 10:00 p.m., we quickly learned the only way we could sustain our hunger until then was to eat a late lunch and follow it with an evening nap. Well rested after the sun went down, we re-emerged from our hotel refreshed and ready to explore the tapas restaurants in the hip neighborhoods of Barri Gotic and El Raval.

Our final night in Barcelona, we joined thousands of locals and tourists to witness the free light show at the majestic Montjuic Fountains. The musical display of colorful lights and water dazzled young and old alike. I was sad to see our quick stop end so soon. In just three days, Barcelona's wide, walkable boulevards, gorgeous architecture, and tasty tapas had lured me back in. I was ready to stay for a month, but instead our plane took off the next day for a new culinary delight—Lyon, France.

Lyon had been on my list of French cities to visit for many years, but it always seemed to be outranked by the likes of Paris, Provence, or Nice. Lyon is not flashy and I think that's intentional. Its residents know its charms well and don't want the outside world to discover them. Spending a week in livable Lyon was an immersion into the French culture full of markets, bouchons, bike rides, and slow living.

As we eased effortlessly into yet another city and began uncovering its individual personality, I was reminded why I loved living in England a decade before. Every European country, though relatively close in proximity, exudes a culture and ambience all its own. And within each country, every city has a signature style. Europeans know what they are good at and they do it well. In Lyon we quickly learned that food was their hallmark. Known as the gastronomic capital of France, dishes were traditional, rich, and a playground for adventurous eaters.

Bouchons are small, local establishments with red and white checkered tablecloths where the owner sits beside you as he describes the myriad of meats he has prepared, often using every organ and body part of each animal. Swimming in sauces and cream, even a timid tourist can dive into delicious plates that don't turn the stomach, but fill it heartily. I tried the *quenelles de brochet* (fish soufflé in a lobster bisque), which became my go-to entrée. Mitch and I sampled duck and pork terrine which—to our delight—was all included in a very reasonable fixed price three-course meal. Never one to shy away from adventurous food, Mitch tasted an amazing pig's cheek and buttery escargot. To save a bit of money and negotiations at the table, we fed Luke earlier at our apartment. He tasted a few bites, albeit unwillingly. Unsurprisingly he preferred the pastries and managed to eat an éclair, croissant, or fresh-baked brioche every day.

Lyon has a brilliant bicycle share program with kiosks all around town. With a small deposit, you can buy a ticket and venture into the labyrinth of city streets and riverside promenades on easy and cheap transportation. To counterbalance our increased caloric intake, we rode for miles along the Saone and Rhone rivers that straddle Lyon's main peninsula. Luke found a favorite riverside playground and played with local children. Several days we explored Parc Tete d'Or, larger than New York City's Central Park and bursting with rose gardens, a lake, and a zoo.

Slowing down in Lyon came as a welcome relief. We disregarded the clock and walked at the pace of the locals. We rose each morning with only the task of visiting the local patisserie across the street for fresh bread and pastries. Some days I walked to the nearby market to buy just-picked apricots and cherries. Every afternoon we tried a different local cheese, paté, and wine. Folding into the French lifestyle seemed embarrassingly cliché but at the same time wonderfully comfortable and easy. It was the perfect precursor to our following weeks of reuniting with family and friends.

We drove south from Lyon and traversed the Alps with a quick jaunt into Switzerland before making our way to Bologna to meet our family for a week in the Italian countryside. Mitch's brother Walker joined us again—this time in the Western Hemisphere— and brought his daughter, Julia, along. Julia is Luke's age and they are not only cousins but dear friends.

Mitch and I were ecstatic for Luke to have a playmate his own age and Luke proclaimed himself Julia's tour guide for the week. He seemed to enjoy showing his cousin the world; this was her first trip out of the United States. We scheduled several excursions during their stay to show Walker and Julia the essence of the Emilia-Romagna district, one of our favorite Italian areas known for its food and fast cars.

During their visit we toured the Ferrari factory, a Parmesan cheese farm, and gelato machine manufacturer complete with its own gelateria for sampling after the factory tour. The dads took Luke and Julia off on their own, leaving me contentedly behind to prepare supper, wash clothes, or read in quiet solitude. Our family dynamic eased gently from three to five as we remembered our extensions like lost appendages reattached.

I learned a lot about my husband and his role as a father on this journey and was able to witness it from afar as he and his brother cared for our children. This generation of dads has gone all in. They have embraced a new era of fatherhood and devote time and energy to be an active part of their kids' lives. They are willing to bear the burden of breadwinner, head of the household, and also involved father. It's a big job. I'm so proud of my husband, my brother-in-law, and our friends who have accepted the challenge with joy and enthusiasm.

For us, parenting has always been a team effort. I envisioned raising a family together with shared responsibilities, and thankfully Mitch agreed. He wanted to be a part of his child's life and that reality had played out as a perfect example in the months we traveled the world together. Was it hard? Yes. Mitch and I were in desperate need of a babysitter to rekindle our intimacy as best friends without our third wheel. But the time that my husband devoted to our son is a gift Luke will have forever. The conversations, experiences, and poignant moments will hopefully be embedded in Luke's memory so that he never has a doubt that both of his parents have invested significantly into his life.

I have watched other parents take time off of work and travel around the country and the world with their kids. The weeks are not spent to relax or fulfill a personal passion or hobby but to invest time with their children making memories. From experience, I know it is a sacrifice. Selfishly, parents sometimes want to be doing their own thing with adult friends and spouses. But I hope these days spent pouring into our children and showing them the world will offer them a fresh perspective on what is out there and how much their parents want to share it with them.

I wasn't sure if we were capable of parenting 24/7 for nine months. It was definitely out of my comfort zone. But Mitch and I counted these memories—both the beautiful and challenging—as highlights of being parents. The time spent with our son understanding his obsessions, likes, and dislikes and spending countless hours together is something we may never do again—certainly not at this sweet age of eight years old. I loved watching him grow, both physically and mentally, seeing him awe-inspired, and enjoying the simple and slow pleasures of life. I may never understand his love of cars and vehicles, and I know I'll never comprehend why he talks incessantly, but I do love him dearly and recognize that our time together during this journey was marked on my heart forever.

TRIP TIP: City share bikes are popping up all over Europe and the United States and are a great way to cover more ground for less money. Investigate the city where you are headed and cycle along the river paths or public parks, avoiding the city streets until you are a pro. And use your time wisely . . . you can get a great deal if you are willing to swap them in and out of kiosks before your price increases.

22

More of Italy and France: Paradise Lost and Found Again

It finally happened. I became tired. Not just sleepy because of another night in a strange, uncomfortable bed. I was tired of traveling. After seven months, I was proud of how far we had come. There were moments when I longed for the comforts of home but the feeling passed quickly as we moved on to our next destination—another adventure around every corner.

But as we sat, ironically, in one of my favorite European cities, I found myself longing for home. We had arrived to our Airbnb apartment in Florence after saying goodbye to Walker and Julia and a fantastic week together. What we expected to be a magical, fourteenth-century flat with views of the Duomo Cathedral was missing a critical element—hot water. Normally, I can last a few days without a shower as evidenced by our WWOOFing exploit. But this time, I lost my patience. After dragging our bags on the cobblestone streets through the burgeoning summer crowds, my relaxed, calm demeanor was shot. I wanted to take a hot shower!

My lousy attitude is commonly known as traveler's burnout, and I had read about it when first researching our trip. Although it was nearly impossible to fathom at the time, I knew there was a good chance the malaise would find me one day. When even the most beautiful sights, sounds, and tastes could not pull me from my frustration and negative attitude, I knew it was time to re-evaluate.

First, I thanked God for our amazing opportunity. I knew He made the entire experience come to life and I was so deeply grateful. What we were experiencing—the good, the bad, and the ugly—were treasures of a lifetime. Already, I began feeling a wee bit better.

Next, I slipped out of the apartment and walked the streets alone to try and wrap my brain around the rich history of the city where we had just arrived. When Leonardo, Raphael, and Donatello were making Florence famous, our country had not yet been discovered. Gazing up at the monstrous Duomo with its stunning green and white façade began to bring my little life back into perspective.

Lastly, I decided to do something I love. After managing restraint (almost) every time Luke enjoyed a decadent gelato, this day I chose to indulge. One of the finest treats in all the world is on every corner in Florence, so I went for it. One cold scoop and my smile began to return. I was ready to tackle whatever came our way on the rest of the crazy adventure. Sometimes even the most genteel and beautiful places tip the balance and throw you to the ledge. I said a quick prayer of thanks that I had managed not to fall too far into the depths of despair and self-pity.

We reunited with our WWOOFing friend Diego while in Florence and his laid back outlook on life continued to draw me out of my dark mood. Diego had left Le Fattizze farm and was housesitting in Florence, hoping to return later in the summer when the campground was in full swing and needed extra working hands.

We said goodbye to Italy for the final time and flew back to France to meet my mom. If you have read any books about the south of France and the vibrant Provençal region, you probably know about the famous fields of lavender that dot the countryside in the Luberon region just east of Avignon. If your timing is just right, the weather cooperates, and you find yourself there in June or July, you are rewarded with heavenly scents from miles and miles of lavender fields in valleys across Provence.

It was one of my mom's dreams to see the lavender and experience the magic of Provence. When Mitch and I were there a decade before, I walked through markets and strolled through quaint villages thinking how much she would love it. So it was sweet serendipity to invite her on our journey and experience Provence with her for the first time.

Luke loved having his "Nana" along on our journey and they laughed together in the backseat of our rental car while Mitch careened around winding roads seeking out the perfectly-purple fields of flowers. We made numerous stops, each one better than the next, and we twirled around the aromatic rows like Maria in the *Sound of Music* hills.

Shopping alongside locals in their weekly market is another quintessential Provençal pastime. Tasting homemade goat cheese, olive tapenade, and freshly-picked fruit as you stroll through picturesque lanes is something that never happens in our life at home. My mother loves to shop, so I knew she would swoon over the scenic artwork, jacquard linens, and lavender soaps, gathering gifts and mementos to take back home.

Her gift to us was offering to babysit several evenings after we had returned from full days of exploring. Mitch and I were thrilled to have a few date nights but found them to be awkward at first, not remembering how to be alone without our child. However, after a glass of wine at the restaurant just around the corner from our apartment where he soundly slept, we eased back into adult conversation and lingered over our precious private outings.

There are a few friends in life who know me inside out. They support, encourage, and celebrate life with me joyfully. My friend, Jordan, is one of those people. She and her husband, Patrick, championed our crazy idea to travel around the world early on and had cheered us to nearly the finish line. So it was only fitting that we crossed paths on our journey and joined them for a week of fun with our two families. I couldn't have asked for a better friend and sweeter family to spend time with, and the idea of relaxing in the south of France wasn't too shabby either! Every morning included a trip to the local *boulangerie* where we eschewed the American diet for croissants, brioche, and baguettes. We embraced outdoor picnics and reveled in the fact that we could enjoy our rosé without fighting bugs or humidity like we endured during hot, sticky summers back home.

Luke was ecstatic to play with Jordan and Patrick's three children, and Mitch and I soaked up quality time with some of our dearest friends. Our time in Southern France seemed to encapsulate some of the best parts of home in a magnificently foreign setting.

Patrick's mother was born in France and her extended family still lives throughout the country. Aunts, uncles, and cousins were descending on the tiny town of Carqueiranne for the annual family reunion. Since our visit coincided, we were happy to join the celebration.

Always looking for opportunities to be a part of a local and authentic experience, Mitch and I offered to play host and hostess for the reunion party so that our friends could enjoy time with relatives they rarely see. We ensured the rosé never stopped flowing and Mitch participated in a spirited game of *petanque* in the gravel driveway with the older patriarchs of the family. Babies were kissed, the children swam under the hot sun in the backyard pool, and the entire family of twenty-three posed for photos in their requisite French *chapeau* hats to commemorate the occasion. From afar, Mitch and I watched as generations of a global family came together on one afternoon to celebrate life, and we felt honored to witness and play a small part in their memories.

TRIP TIP: Before you build your itinerary for Provence, spend some time researching each of the town's traditional market days. Local markets happen once or twice a week on different days for each town. To avoid missing one you want to visit, plan your driving route in advance around the markets you intend to see.

23

England: Where the Wanderlust Began

We bid our friends *adieu*, promising to see them back in America in six weeks. We had saved our second home—my favorite city in the world—for our final destination. London was the place Mitch and I learned to live abroad and our journey came full circle when we returned there as seasoned global travelers.

My greatest desire was to replant our roots—however temporary—in our former hometown of Richmond in Southwest London. Set along the Thames River, twelve miles outside of London, Richmond is a village worth visiting if you have already seen London's major sites and want to experience a slower pace of life just outside the city.

Because our budget was also nearing its end, we strategically researched housesitting opportunities to afford us a free place to stay. After months of trolling TrustedHousesitters.com listings, I connected with an American expat family living in Richmond who was traveling back to the United States for a two-week holiday. They needed house sitters to care for their two pet dogs and we agreed to the responsibilities and free accommodation—a perfect arrangement.

We fell in love with Lola and Piper, an English and Irish Setter whose lives centered around daily walks in glorious Richmond Park. The vast green space is the largest royal park in London, originally

King Charles I's hunting ground and still home to hundreds of
striking deer and other wildlife.

Settling into our daily routine, we traversed miles and miles
through the park with the dogs. We walked them two or three
times a day and enjoyed the local life of Richmond's town center
in between. We visited our favorite pubs and restaurants, walked
Luke by our old flat, and bought picnic sundries at Marks and
Spencer grocery store for outdoor suppers in the park with the dogs.
On Sundays, we returned to the church where Mitch and I were
members a decade before. Though no one recognized us, we felt
right at home.

In recent years Lola had gone blind, so she was usually bound
to her leash and timidly followed behind whomever was walking her
for fear of the unknown. Her sister Piper was spry and energetic but
highly trained. We allowed Piper to run off her leash when we were
in the large confines of the park and she always faithfully returned,
tail wagging, whenever we called her name.

The three of us loved having dogs in our lives again. (We had
lost our golden retriever five years earlier to old age.) Luke seemed to
find comradery and a certain companionship to the dogs instantly,
and they to him. We all became lovingly attached and found it hard
to leave them when our two-week job came to an end.

During our housesitting stay, we celebrated Mitch's birthday
with a quintessential English pastime—tennis at Wimbledon. A
little known secret to entry during the fortnight of play, visitors
can gain access to day tickets each afternoon after 5:00 p.m. for
a mere twenty pounds. While these tickets do not admit you into
Centre Court, Court One, or Two, visitors can squeeze into any
available seats to see other matches throughout the grounds or join
hundreds of local Londoners spread out on the hill behind Centre
Court to watch the action on giant TV screens. It's a great way to
experience the famous tournament without breaking the bank and
we celebrated Mitch's forty-second birthday watching Andy Murray

battle his way toward the semi-final match, and ultimately to victory as Wimbledon champion.

I counted our two weeks in Richmond as one of the greatest blessings on our trip. Richmond is a town that has my heart and it would have been impossible to afford accommodations for any length of time without a housesitting job. We lived like the locals we once were, reminded why we love this little slice of heaven in England.

We met several other expats when we lived and worked in London, but most had since moved back to their home countries as we had. One of my closest friends, however, was Welsh. Although she and her English husband left the city soon after we did, they settled in the idyllic city of Bath just two hours outside of London. We rode the train to reunite and spend a weekend with them and their two boys, who were close in age to Luke.

Before any of us had children, Lauren and Alistair were the friends we could always count on for a fun—and sometimes crazy—night out in London. Al, an advertising executive, and Lauren, a public relations colleague at Coca-Cola, always seemed to know of the newest restaurant or most popular club. One memorable night a decade ago, we found ourselves dancing with one of the Spice Girls, sipping champagne in a VIP lounge with famous English footballers, and having our photos snapped by the paparazzi. Oh, how times change.

We arrived at the Bath train station and were met by Lauren and her two boys, Ben and Sam, who had just been picked up from school. We embraced after two long years since our last visit and settled into their house on the hill overlooking the historic Roman city while the boys began playing with Legos.

"How have you been, love?" Lauren asked, boiling a kettle of water for our tea. "We've been following your travels and cannot believe you finally made it to see us after all these months."

Mitch and I shared our recent exploits and enjoyed relaxing in our friends' comfortable home.

"Al and I have a surprise for you!" Lauren exclaimed. "Tomorrow we are going to take all of the boys to an amusement park so that you two can have a day alone at the spa."

Bath is known for its natural, warm waters that have drawn visitors from around the world since ancient times in search of rejuvenation and healing. We had never experienced the eponymous waters on previous visits to Bath and the thought of a relaxing day together was more gracious than I could have imagined.

"Are you sure?" I asked, knowing that a day out with three boys would be the exact opposite of relaxation for Al and Lauren.

"Absolutely!" she replied. "We have already told the boys and they can't wait to spend the day with Luke. And we can't either."

Instead of a late night clubbing with our friends, we woke early the next morning to see them off for a day of amusement rides and kid-centered fun. Mitch and I checked into Thermae Bath Spa after a leisurely lunch and spent the afternoon soaking in hot pools and sweating in aromatic steam rooms. It was the most luxurious excursion we had had in nine months. Our dear friends still knew how to show us a great time!

Our final weeks in England were notably centered around London and all it has to offer. It was Luke's third trip to our favorite city but we found a never-ending list of activities to keep us busy. London can be an expensive destination but we were blessed to stay in a friend's vacant flat since she had recently moved back to the United States and it was still on the market to sell.

There are plenty of free—or very inexpensive—activities all around London to suit many interests and all ages. We started with our favorites and then explored new and lesser-known sites. I believe a visit to London should always include a walk around Big Ben, Buckingham Palace, and Piccadilly Circus. But after the more crowded, touristy sites, there are a myriad of equally interesting spots that get you off the well-trodden path. The summer season is especially packed with events and festivals that are family friendly and oftentimes free.

One of our first destinations whenever we arrive in London is the Borough Market, situated on the South Bank of the river Thames near Shakespeare's Globe Theater and London Bridge. Walking through the stalls of local food purveyors is a beautiful picture of London's diversity. Foods from all over the world make their home here and we enjoyed tasting everything from Indian curry to Gloustershire cheese in the historic market under the bridge.

We always take advantage of the free museums in the city, making time to visit The National Gallery, The Science Museum, and the British Museum—a few of our family favorites. After reading about it for years and finally making the hour-long trip north on the Underground, Luke loved seeing airplanes up close at the Royal Air Force museum. Even though it is outside the city center, the museum was easily accessible and we spent hours gazing at the historic aircraft and reading courageous war stories.

One afternoon, we took the public ferry down the Thames River to Greenwich. While the small village boasts the Prime Meridian, there is much more to see including the historic Cutty Sark ship, the free Maritime Museum full of seaborne artifacts, and the Royal Observatory with a view of the stars. We discovered "Free Tours By Foot" offered an excellent free walking tour with fascinating stories and history. We were so impressed that we joined a few of their other tours in the city later that week. Most people don't give Greenwich the time it deserves, but our family loved it and spent an entire day exploring all it had to offer.

Between visits to museums, Mitch and I were always on the lookout for the fantastic playgrounds hiding throughout London to let Luke run off some energy. He loved the unique playscapes with climbing towers and zip lines that are surprisingly daring compared to what we have at home. Mitch and I enjoyed chatting with local parents or other visiting families while the kids found universal enjoyment on the playground no matter where they had come from.

Although technically only for kids over fourteen, we also revisited our proven pastime of family bicycling, this time with London's popular share bike scheme. We rode through the connecting Hyde, Green, and St. James' parks and found ourselves in town for the annual RideLondon Bike Day. The city closed down many of its streets to vehicle traffic and we pedaled past all of the famous landmarks with other cycling Londoners and tourists.

London has so much to offer that we found it hard—as we always do—to accomplish everything we love in the limited time we were there. It's a city I could visit a thousand times and never see it all. But its familiarity gave us the sense of being at home and we began to transition back to that which we were accustomed.

TRIP TIP: Before you cross the pond, apply your children under age sixteen for the Oyster Zip card online so they can travel for free on the London Underground, known as the Tube, and buses throughout the city.

24

How to Go Home

As the sun began to set, Mitch, Luke, and I sat on a blanket in Hyde Park reflecting and reminiscing about our journey—the people we had met, places we saw, new foods we tried, and new adventures that pushed us past our comfort zones and out of our rut. We began the heavy task of processing our experiences and trying to make sense of it all before we returned to our "traditional" life in the United States.

We savored countless memories—both personal and collective—that defined our trip. Because we traveled light, the souvenirs we carried home were not physical objects but goals for our family. We pledged to embrace the slow and simple joys of life—taking hikes, bike rides, and visiting waterfalls. We vowed to visit our neighborhood farmers market and buy fresh fruit and vegetables from locals instead of from a mega grocery store. We desired to make recipes from our cooking schools and read more books instead of watching TV. We wanted to give back where we live—serving others instead of ourselves. By adding these activities to our routine back home, we hoped these souvenirs would help us remember and honor our experience of traveling around the globe. I knew it wouldn't be easy as we re-entered our busy lives with work, school, friends, and family. But consciously choosing to live simply amidst an American life of busyness would keep us permanently out of our rut and continue to grow us as individuals and as a family.

Our goal of getting out of our comfort zone had been achieved, and we learned many things in the process. The most encouraging discovery was that people all over the world are inherently kind. No matter where we found ourselves, strangers were friendly and helpful to visitors in their country; often stopping to lend a hand or engage our son in friendly conversation. As Americans traveling abroad, we learned not to be afraid or feel as though we were in danger. Of course we were careful and "street smart" as any tourist should be, but the world we saw was a safe and friendly place.

We also learned that stretching made us stronger. We pushed ourselves in more ways than one—volunteering, staying in accommodations that weren't our normal standard, and learning new languages to immerse ourselves with new friends and cultures. I learned that stretching yourself on a daily basis is good for the soul as well as the brain. Luke was more confident and independent now that he had walked into the classroom of the world. Mitch and I had broken down long-held stereotypes and dusted off the cobwebs in our brains while traversing and communicating in multiple countries. The experience was richer because at times we got uncomfortable and now we were stronger people for it.

I was happy to learn that we were able to stick to our travel budget. You do not have to win the lottery to travel around the globe. We knew that the American dollar would stretch further in places like Southeast Asia and India but were pleasantly surprised at how little we had to spend for great accommodations and food even in European countries like Croatia and Turkey. In the world's sharing economy, websites like Airbnb offer much lower prices than traditional hotels and it's possible to travel on virtually nothing if you volunteer through organizations like WWOOF or Trusted Housesitters. If you have a desire to see the world, don't let cash be your obstacle.

We also encountered firsthand how magnificent the world's beauty is. It is easy to see why there are several "Wonders of the World" lists. Our planet is exquisite and we witnessed awe-inspiring displays, both natural and man-made. I realized that when I'm at home I don't look up and behold the world around me. Journeying to some of the most remarkable places on Earth reminded me that we live in a place that should delight and inspire us every day.

What I thought would be an epic nine-month journey around the world felt more like a quick trip that was the first of many. Seeing the world opened my eyes to how much more there is to explore and how much I love to travel. I learned that we should never wait for an opportunity to find us—it may never come. We have to go after it.

Seeing your dreams—whatever those dreams may be—through to fruition is one of life's most rewarding experiences. It could be starting a new business or career, trying a new hobby, or beginning to earnestly pursue a lifelong passion. Whatever that certain something is that has you thinking, *I'll do that when I retire/have more money/have more time,* I challenge you to say it out loud to your spouse or a friend today. Once you have spoken it, you will find it is more real and attainable and you can even start planning. Don't stop fulfilling your dreams because life is getting in the way. Make your dreams a part of your life and it will become the one you were meant to live.

We boarded the airplane at Heathrow International early the next morning with heavy but expectant hearts. We were leaving behind our worldly adventures, but the love of family and friends was waiting on the other side of the pond. Luke cried with mixed emotions, and I understood well. I had experienced this dichotomy when we left England after our two years living abroad. It's difficult to leave behind something you dearly love yet be present anticipating the happy return home.

As we flew over the Atlantic, I sat in disbelief at what we had accomplished and my heart overflowed with gratitude. I was so thankful to have a marriage partner who appreciated adventure and who wasn't afraid to live outside the normal expectations of society.

I was immensely grateful that our son fully embraced our journey and had learned so much about the marvelous world in which we live. Also to be appreciated, we had not been sick a single day on our trip and we had been protected from theft, injury, and harm. These were gifts—plain and simple. I continued to be awestruck by God's amazing provision for us—His arms of safety, His people welcoming us throughout the world, and His Spirit of patience and joy that filled us day after day. I recognized that something larger than the three of us was in control of our lives, not only during the past nine months, but also in whatever lay ahead. And so, that is where I put my focus as we flew west for the final time.

EPILOGUE

Last week we realized it had been nine months since our homecoming. We have been back as long as we were gone. It's hard to believe.

Luke transitioned beautifully back into his life, joyfully launching into third grade thanks to the sweet embrace of teachers, coaches, and friends just two weeks after we moved back into our house. His natural re-entry surprised me. Although we reminisce daily about our travels, he adjusted quite well to our life back in America.

Mitch was offered a job with his former company and began a few short days after our return. Pragmatic as always, he attacked his role at work with gusto and accepted the recurrence of our routines matter-of-factly. He was happy to see our bank account replenished and willingly began traveling for work every week to restock our depleted rewards accounts. Within a few months he had already accumulated enough SkyMiles to book a family trip to Belize the following spring. It was a concerted effort to keep traveling to new places out of our comfort zone whenever possible.

I found a new confidence and passion for writing after journaling and keeping a blog of our travels. Although I went back to work part-time, I spent my days off in our local library penning what would become this memoir. It was cathartic to revisit our experiences from start to finish and I found my mind was often not on the routine tasks at home, but in far-flung destinations like Vietnam, Croatia, or Kenya.

We love being back home, but some days I wish there was a new country to explore or a new adventure to experience. Instead of traveling—for now—we are investing in where we live. We devote our time to giving back to others and seek to get out of our comfort zone in our own zip code. When your heart desires exploration and new experiences but your circumstances keep you grounded, I have found that serving and giving help stretch me to those places of joy and contentment in a similar way traveling does. For now, that is my focus.

Many people asked if we considered our journey a success, and I would say resoundingly, "Yes!" But it wasn't because of anything we accomplished, achieved, or experienced. We deemed it successful because we trusted in God. We began living in deep dependence on Him for everything—for doors to open so the trip could happen, for introductions to enrich our experiences with people we had never met, for travel safety, and health. That trust and willingness to relinquish control gave me a confidence to follow our dreams and expect great things to unfold.

People usually associate success with perfection, not falling or stumbling, not making mistakes. But through problems and setbacks—not only on our journey around the world, but in everyday life—we were confronted with the need to rely more on God. He is bigger and better than anything we can do on our own and that was beautifully displayed on the global stage when everything seemed unfamiliar, distant, and new.

I believe God knew our hearts' desire to experience the world outside of our hometown. When He opened the doors for us, trust and dependence followed. Because of our faith, we experienced a journey that took us thousands of miles around the world but immensely closer to each other and to God.

REFERENCE AND RECOMMENDATION GUIDE

Here are a few of our favorite places and activities, as well as websites that were helpful to us during our journey. We are not affiliated with any of them. We just want to pass along our great experiences to you!

New Zealand
- Auckland
  o Museum of Transportation and Technology (MOTAT) - www.motat.org.nz
  o Cable Bay Vineyards - cablebay.nz
  o Mud Brick Vineyards - www.mudbrick.co.nz
  o Te Motu Vineyards - www.temotu.co.nz
- Cambridge
  o Waitamo glow worm caves with Spellbound Tours - www.glowworm.co.nz
- Napier
  o Mission Estate Winery - www.missionestate.co.nz
  o Church Road Wines - www.church-road.co.nz
  o Bicycle rental - www.bikehirenapier.co.nz

Australia
- Melbourne
  o I'm Free walking tour - www.imfree.com.au/melbourne
  o Patch café - patchcafe.com.au
  o Healesville Sanctuary - www.zoo.org.au/healesville

- o   Yering Station Winery - www.yering.com
- o   Hargreaves Hill Brewing Company - hargreaveshill.com.au
- o   Yarra Valley Chocolaterie - www.yvci.com.au
- ▪ Cairns
  - o   Compass Cruise snorkeling and dive excursions - compasscruises.com.au
- ▪ Sydney
  - o   Bondi Beach Icebergs pool and club - icebergs.com.au/swimming-pool
  - o   4 Pines Brewery - 4pinesbeer.com.au
  - o   I'm Free walking tour - www.imfree.com.au/sydney
  - o   Australian National Maritime Museum - www.anmm.gov.au
  - o   Royal Botanic Gardens - www.rbgsyd.nsw.gov.au

Thailand
- ▪ Bangkok
  - o   Yaowarat street food tour - www.bangkokfoodtours.com/chinatown
  - o   Thip Samai (best pad thai in the city!) - 313 Th Maha Chai, Pranakorn, Bangkok
  - o   Golden Mango restaurant - 1340-2 Charoen Krung Road, Bangkok
- ▪ Chiang Mai
  - o   Eagle Track zip line tours - www.eagletrackchiangmai.com
  - o   Elephant Nature Park - elephantnaturepark.org
  - o   Zabb E Lee Cooking School - www.zabbeleecooking.com
- ▪ Koh Yao Noi
  - o   Lom Lae Resort - www.lomlae.com

Cambodia
- Siem Reap
  - The Villa Siem Reap - www.thevillasiemreap.com
  - My Little Café - Tepvong Street, Siem Reap
  - Driver Marom Hem - www.maromhem.wordpress.com
  - Free tour of silk farm - www.artisansdangkor.com
  - Le Tigre de Papier cooking school - letigredepapier.com

Vietnam
- Hoi An
  - Magnolia Garden homestay - magnoliagardenvilla.com
  - Banh Mi Phuong restaurant - 2B Phan Chau Trinh, Hoi An
  - Thuan Tinh cooking school - cooking-tour.com
  - Free bicycle tour - www.hoianfreetour.com
- Hanoi
  - Hanoi Kids free walking tours - hanoikids.org
  - Street food tour - www.hanoistreetfoodtour.com
  - Bun Cha Ta restaurant - www.bunchata.com
- Hue
  - Free walking tour - www.beebeetravel.com

China
- Hong Kong
  - Free walking tour - hkfreewalk.com
  - Science Museum - hk.science.museum
  - Museum of History - hk.history.museum
  - Maritime Museum - www.hkmaritimemuseum.org/eng/

India
- Jaipur
  - Pearl Palace hotel - hotelpearlpalace.com
  - Cooking school - www.jaipurcookingclasses.com
  - Free walking tour - www.freetour.com/jaipur/free-jaipur-walking-tour

Kenya
- Nairobi
  - First Love orphanage - www.firstloveinternational.com
- Maasai Mara
  - Ilkeliani safari lodge - www.ilkeliani.com

Egypt
- Cairo
  - Private tour guide - Ashraf Maksoud, perfectguide@hotmail.com

Turkey
- Istanbul
  - Basilica Cistern - www.yerebatan.com
  - Hagia Sofia - www.ayasofyamuzesi.gov.tr
  - Donerci Sahin Usta restaurant - www.donercisahinusta.com
  - Topkapi Palace - www.topkapisarayi.gov.tr
  - Free walking tour - www.istanbul-freetour.com/daily-tours/free-tour/
- Cappadocia
  - Divan Cave hotel - www.divancavehouse.com/eng/
  - Hot air balloon ride - www.butterflyballoons.com/en/home/
  - ATV rental - www.silkroadrentacar.com
- Selçuk
  - Hotel Nilya - www.nilya.com

Croatia
- Zagreb
  - Free walking tour - www.freetour.com/zagreb/free-spirit-walking-tour
- Istria
  - Mondo Konoba - Barbacan 1, Motovun
  - Matosevic Winery - www.matosevic.com

- o Kabola Winery - www.kabola.hr
- o Kozlovic Winery - www.kozlovic.hr

Bosnia
- Sarajevo
  - o Free walking tour - www.sarajevowalkingtours.com

Italy
- Puglia
  - o Le Fattizze farm - lefattizze.it
- Sicily
  - o Leonardo DaVinci Museum, Syracuse - www. leonardoarchimede.com
  - o Caffe Sicilia (best cannoli) – Corso Vittorio Emanuele, 125, Noto
- Emilia-Romagna
  - o Ferrari factory tour - www.musei.ferrari.com
  - o Parmesan farm tour -www.parmigianoreggiano.com/ where/guided_tours_dairies_1/
  - o Carpigiani gelato factory tour - www.gelatomuseum.com

Spain
- Barcelona
  - o Gaudi walking tour - runnerbeantours.com/tours/ gaudi-free-tour-barcelona/
  - o La Sagrada Familia - www.sagradafamilia.org
  - o Montjuic fountain show - irbarcelona.org/ barcelona-tourist-attractions/magic-fountain-montjuic/

France
- Lyon
  - o Le Musee bouchon - 2 rue des Forces, Lyon
  - o Chez Hugon bouchon - www.bouchonlyonnais.fr
  - o Ride share bicycles - velov.grandlyon.com/en.html

- Provence
  - o Avignon share bicycles - www.smoove-bike.com/avignon
  - o Luberon bicycle rental - rouelibre.luberon@gmail.com
  - o Domaine des Peyre Winery - www.domainedespeyre.com

England
- Bath
  - o Thermae Bath Spa - www.thermaebathspa.com
- London
  - o Borough Market - www.boroughmarket.org.uk
  - o The National Gallery - www.nationalgallery.org.uk
  - o Science Museum - www.sciencemuseum.org.uk
  - o British Museum - www.britishmuseum.org
  - o RAF Museum - www.rafmuseum.org.uk/london/
  - o Greenwich Museums - www.rmg.co.uk
  - o Free walking tours - www.freetoursbyfoot.com/london-tours/
  - o RideLondon Bike Day - www.prudentialridelondon.co.uk/events/freecycle/
  - o Oyster travel card - tfl.gov.uk/fares-and-payments/travel-for-under-18s/zip-oyster-photocards

www.RutToTheLedge.com
www.HuffingtonPost.com/author/suzanne-rutledge
www.BootsnAll.com
www.ExtraPackofPeanuts.com
www.NomadicMatt.com
www.RickSteves.com
www.TrustedHousesitters.com
www.WWOOF.net
www.Airbnb.com

ACKNOWLEDGEMENTS

This book would not be possible without the adventure itself, and for that I want to thank my best friend and love of my life, my husband Mitch. He dreamed with me and put the plan into action by booking planes, trains, and automobiles while keeping our budget on track so we could enjoy every moment of the journey. He continues to support our family with selfless love and humble leadership. He encouraged me to put our story on paper, not just for posterity but to share and encourage other families to follow their dreams like we did.

I'm so grateful to be a mom, and I want to thank Luke for his joyful, adventurous spirit. He loves to learn and has a contagious positivity that is vital when traveling the globe. Thank you, Luke, for being our constant encourager and a beautiful light in this world.

When I decided to write this book, I was encouraged by a friend to form an editorial team and they have faithfully read and critiqued each chapter. Thank you for sacrificing your time and offering invaluable input Mary Beth and Brent Cole, Laura Cushing, Justin Honaman, Laura Brightwell, and Tammy Shoemaker.

Before I recruited my editorial team, I knew a prayer team was an equally, if not more essential cog in the wheel. These ladies prayed alongside me every step of our actual journey and then through the writing process. I love you and appreciate your friendship Leslie Barron, Jessica Condit, Mary DeLoach, Katie Ryan, Jordan Sneed, and Robin Stewart.

We are so grateful for our friends around the world who welcomed us into their homes with open arms—the Gillies and Griessels in Australia, the Van Den Bergs in Hong Kong, and the Sneeds in France. Thank you, Laura, for offering your beautiful flat in London and to the Bryans who loved on us in Bath. To the Staniers and the wonderful night in Oxfordshire, thank you. Thanks also to my cousin, Rebecca, who met up with us in England and, more importantly, coined our family's travel moniker, From the Rut to the Ledge.